Take God's Hand
and You Will Never Walk Alone

Take God's Hand and You Will Never Walk Alone

Poems, Prayers, and Promises

By NEAL ERVIN

RESOURCE *Publications* • Eugene, Oregon

TAKE GOD'S HAND AND YOU WILL NEVER WALK ALONE
Poems, Prayers, and Promises

Copyright © 2020 Neal Ervin. All rights reserved. Except for brief quotations in critical publications or reviews, no part of this book may be reproduced in any manner without prior written permission from the publisher. Write: Permissions, Wipf and Stock Publishers, 199 W. 8th Ave., Suite 3, Eugene, OR 97401.

Resource Publications
An Imprint of Wipf and Stock Publishers
199 W. 8th Ave., Suite 3
Eugene, OR 97401

www.wipfandstock.com

PAPERBACK ISBN: 978-1-7252-6019-1
HARDCOVER ISBN: 978-1-7252-6018-4
EBOOK ISBN: 978-1-7252-6020-7

Manufactured in the U.S.A.   FEBRUARY 6, 2020

Contents

Permissions | IX
Preface | XV
Introduction | XIX

God Loves You | 1
Life's Pathway is Not a Road Race | 3
Breath of Hope and Life | 5
Another Blessed Day | 7
Arise and Reach Out to Jesus | 9
You are with Me Always | 11
Reach for God's Perfection | 13
Cheer Up and Let God Lighten your Burdens | 15
Do Not Give Up—Stay the Course | 17
Take Control Lord—Lead Me | 19
God Calling Earth—God to Earth—Come in Earth | 21
More Life Forevermore—A Prayer | 23
Redial God—Do not Hang Up on life. | 25
My Rock—My All—Forever | 27
Lead Me Everyday | 29
The Godsent Touch of Love—Pass it On | 31
The Ultimate Best Friend Forever | 33
You are Never Alone—With Christ | 35
Let Go of the Past | 37
A Prayer to Stand Tall for Jesus | 39
Amazing Grace IOU— Endless Love | 41
My Day Your Way | 43
Spiritual Friend—Heaven Sent | 45
Keep Me from Temptation | 47
Let Life Heal and Grow Again | 49

Arise and Walk with God | 51
A Prayer of Thanks | 53
The Spiritual Renewal of Life | 55
Sister to Sister—Our Loves Lives Forever | 57
Feel the Fullness in His Care | 59
Goodbye Mortal Hello Angel | 61
Do Your Best Always | 63
The Choice Test | 65
Faith and Trust = Synergy | 67
Comfort Zone—On the Narrow Holy Road | 69
A Forever God Season—In Perpetual Light | 71
Jehovah Rapha has The Rx for Healing | 73
Transcendent Love | 75
Awesome Faith—Never Lose It | 77
Let Go and Trust God | 79
Exalt and Praise His Name | 81
Sow Seeds for a Joyful Harvest | 83
Seek God First—Trust Him | 85
Let God Decide | 87
Mirror Image | 89
Soar on His Wings | 91
Stay Positive—Keep Moving On | 93
Time Brings Brighter Days. | 95
A Prayer for Blessings and Guidance | 97
Keep Me Today and Always—A Prayer | 99
Patience and Virtue—A Recipe for Life | 101
Call on The Lord for Restoration | 103
God Bless Our Home | 105
Hold on to the Lovelight—of The Cross | 107
A True—Life Miracle Story | 109
A New Life Portrait in Living Light—By God the Master Artist | 112
A Friend + A Buddy = A Fuddy | 114
Mercy and Compassion—Praise Him | 116
Together Always—Never Alone | 118
Sunbeam Smile—Happy Birthday | 120
Take My Hand | 122
Farewell My Brother | 124
Keep the Faith—Ride Life's Tide | 126
True Love Lives On | 128
Thank You for More Than Enough—Everyday | 130

Choose Eternity Wisely | 132
Ingredients for a Happy Life—A Prayer | 134
Angels of The Heavenly King—On Earth | 136
You Get to Choose Your State of Mind | 138
The Blessings of True Love Await | 140
Loving Like God Loves—One Blood | 142
Peace Be unto You—A Prayer of Thanks. | 145
The Blood of Forgiveness—A Prayer | 147
Jesus is Always There | 149
You are My Everything—A Prayer | 151
A New Praise Song—Love Song Prayer | 153
Spiritual Sight—The Love Walk | 155
Universal Soldiers—In the Service of The King | 157
A Good Day Every Day | 159
I See—Through the Eyes of his Word | 161
Happy | 163
The Church of Mankind | 165
Real Living—In the Spirit | 168
Restored—Why I Sing Praises | 170
Leave a Legacy of God's Love | 172
Stay with Me Forever Lord— Another Prayer | 174
Princes & Princess'—Children of the Most High | 176
Do Not Ever Forget God | 178
In Search of the Great I AM | 180
THANX | 182
Walking Hand in Hand—With God | 184

Permissions

Bible scripture taken from:
King James Version—Scriptures marked KJV are taken from the KING JAMES VERSION (KJV): KING JAMES VERSION, public domain.

New Living Translation –Scripture quotations marked NLT are taken from the Holy Bible, New Living Translation, copyright © 1996, 2004, 2015 by Tyndale House Foundation. Used by permission of Tyndale House Publishers, Inc., Carol Stream, Illinois 60188. All rights reserved.

New International Version—Scriptures marked NIV are taken from the NEW INTERNATIONAL VERSION (NIV):

Scripture taken from THE HOLY BIBLE, NEW INTERNATIONAL VERSION ®. Copyright© 1973, 1978, 1984, 2011 by Biblica, Inc.™. Used by permission of Zondervan

English Standard Version—Scripture quotations are from the ESV® Bible (The Holy Bible, English Standard Version®), copyright © 2001 by Crossway, a publishing ministry of Good News Publishers. Used by permission. All rights reserved."

The following quotes were used by permission:

"No matter what storm you face, you need to know that God loves you. He has not abandoned you."
Rev. Franklin Graham
Permissions from Billy Graham Evangelistic Association

***

"The breath of life is divine grace of God."
Lailah Gifty Akita
Permission from Dr. Mrs. Lailah Gifty Akita.

Permissions

***

"When you accept the fact that sometimes seasons are dry
and times are hard and that God is in control of both,
 you will discover a sense of divine refuge, because the
hope then is in God and not in yourself."
Charles R. Swindoll
Excerpted from Avoiding Stress Fractures by Charles R. Swindoll. Copyright © 1990, 1995 by Charles R. Swindoll, Inc. All rights reserved worldwide. Used by permission. insight.org

***

"Expect your every need to be met.
Expect the answer to every problem,
expect abundance on every level."
Eileen Caddy-Permission from Johnathan Caddy—Findhorn Foundation. The Park, Findhorn, IV36

***

"Even though you may want to move forward in your life,
you may have one foot on the brakes. In order to be free,
we must learn how to let go. Release the hurt. Release the fear.
Refuse to entertain your old pain.
The energy it takes to hang onto the past is holding you back
from a new life. What is it you would let go of today?"
Mary Manin Morrissey
From Mary Manin Morrissey, Author of Building your Field of Dreams. Used by permission

***

"I firmly believe that in every situation, no matter how
difficult, God extends grace greater than the hardship,
and strength and peace of mind that can lead us to a
place higher than where we were before."
Andy Griffith
Permission from Guidepost.

***

"To live in the light of a new day and an unimaginable and
unpredictable future, you must become fully present to a
deeper truth—not a truth from your head, but a truth from
 your heart; not a truth from your ego, but a truth from the

Permissions

highest source."
Debbie Ford
Permission from the Ford Institute.

***

"A real friend is one who walks in
when the rest of the world walks out."
Walter Winchell
Permission from American Heritage Publishing

***

"God is in the sadness and the laughter,
in the bitter and the sweet."
Neale Donald Walsch
Permission from Neale Donald Walsch

***

"The irony of the human condition is that it is the narrow
gate to life. Few find it because they are too fearful to look."
Robert J Blizzard
Permission from R. J. Blizzard

***

"The greatest legacy you can pass on to your children and grandchildren is not your money or the other material things you have accumulated in life. The greatest legacy you can pass on to them is the legacy of your character and your faith."
Rev Billy Graham
Permission from Billy Graham Evangelistic Association

***

"But I came to learn that God never shows us something
we aren't ready to understand. Instead, he lets us see
what we need to see, when we are ready to see it.
He'll wait until our eyes and hearts are open to him, and then when we're ready, he will plant our feet on the path that's best for us, but it's up to us to do the walking."
Immaculee Llibagiza
Permission from Immaculée Ilibagiza, LLC

***

"Look in the mirror, go ahead and look yet again.

Permissions

And look not at the reflection, for while this body of
yours is marvelously complex in ways that continue
to elude the reach of modern science, it is but a
simple shell that holds the image of God within you.
And if the shell is that grand, how much more what
God has placed inside."
Craig D. Lounsbrough
Permission from Craig D. Lounsbrough, M.Div., LPC

***

"Be true to yourself, help others, make each day your masterpiece,
make friendship a fine art, drink deeply from good books, especially the
Bible, build a shelter against a rainy day, give thanks for your blessings
and pray for guidance every day."
John Wooden
From—*WOODEN: A Lifetime of Observations and Reflections* (Contemporary)
By permission.

***

"God is the Master Artist painting the picture
of your life, and he sees the whole canvas."
Elisa Pulliam
From—*Unblinded Faith: Gaining Spiritual Sight through Believing God's Word*,
by Elisa Pulliam 2018 By permission.

***

"I will love the light for it shows me the way, yet I will
endure the darkness because it shows me the stars."
Og Mandino
Permission from Og Mandino Office

***

"The Universal Brotherhood of man is our most precious possession,
what there is of it."
Mark Twain
Permission from CMG Worldwide

***

"A regenerated person should have an unspeakable peace in his spirit."
Watchman Nee
Permission from Living Stream Ministry Publications

Permissions

***

"But the Lord watches over us every moment of every day. He is there and He cares about every step and every breath."
Dillon Burroughs—Hunger No More, (c) 2012
Published by New Hope. Used by permission.

***

"We do not segment our lives, giving some time to God, some to our business or schooling, while keeping parts to ourselves. The idea is to live all of our lives in the presence of God, under the authority of God, and for the honor and glory of God. That is what the Christian life is all about."
R.C. Sproul
Permission from Ligonier Ministries

Preface

I was a young Reporter, enroute to Fleet Street London to study journalism.
My father's sudden death changed my life forever.
I put my pen down and walked away from God's purpose for my life.
The many years of pain, loss and heartache that followed would bring me back full circle.
Years later, far away from my Mother I grieved her passing,
holding on to hope in seeing her again one day in heaven.
Six years later my youngest brother suddenly passed away leaving me to wonder about my own mortality.
In just a few years to follow my younger brother was diagnosed with cancer.
The doctors said he had less than 6 months to live.
I felt like I was losing everyone close to me.
I watched his suffering and the determination of his faith and remembered God.
I started praying again, reading my Bible, a gift from my Mom.
I kept faith and hope in Gods' promises as I read his word.
My brother believed God would heal him, against all odds.
We both knew then; we were asking for a miracle.
I started to write again after many years.
The encouragement from my brother and his belief in God literally brought me back to the God of our childhood, and my love for writing.
God heard our prayers. My brother was miraculously healed, leaving the doctors puzzled.
God had my attention, showing me miracle after miracle in the years to follow.
The happiness was short lived when I received the news of my only sister, the youngest of our diminishing clan suddenly passing away.
I had not seen my sister for many years. Now it was too late.
I had so much regret. The pain from the years past came back with the flood of memories.

Preface

Yet, more and more I realized that God was leading me through, walking with me all the way.
I kept writing, praying, believing and embraced a new found friendship with my brother as we became best friends.
Then I lost them both.
God quietly called him home to heaven.
He died peacefully in his sleep almost ten years after his healing.
The year that followed was painful, my best friend , my brother was gone.
My family was gone, I felt as though I had no one, the loneliness was the most painful part.
I lost my hearing to add to it all. I had to learn to live in a different world.
It was scary. I even became fearful of dying.
I met a lot of God's people on the way here, his angels.
I also felt the sting of man's cruelty to man.
I became even closer to God— He gave me strength.
Two years followed and my elderly neighbor and dear friend was diagnosed with cancer.
I rallied to her side, forgetting myself, my pain now paled by her suffering.
Sitting with her in the reception area at the cancer center, I saw the devastation firsthand.
The loss and desolation left by death was everywhere.
The epidemic of wounded souls left to carry on, was even worse.
The grief and sorrow opened my own wounds. I worked on my book while I waited on her at the cancer hospital.
I shared the comfort that God brought to me with others whenever I could.
I knew God was the only one who could fill the void for those who suffer.
Sharing my testimony with others, helped me too.
After 3 years battling cancer, my aged and tired friend passed away.
I wrote a book during the prior years but never finished it, the volume of my poems, penned in rough times was growing and has become this book of poems, prayers and promises.
God led me through the years of loss and heartache to redeem my purpose and fulfill my existence. I had to share the goodness, the strength and joy I received during those years.
He brought me back full circle 40 years later. He is still restoring me.
With prayer, I put this book in his hands and he led me to a publisher in WIPF & STOCK, against all odds.
I am glad I took God's hand and did not let go. His mighty hand never failed me. Not once.

Preface

I hope and pray to God that this book will be a blessing to everyone who suffers, pain, grief and loneliness through loss, death, betrayal and rejection or abandonment, those weakened and cast down by addictions, disabilities and man's inhumanity to man.

Everything becomes life. We must be strong and courageous to overcome what we are faced with. It is not so difficult when we believe that God gives us comfort through the Holy Spirit.

We are not alone, we become strong when we embrace God and learn to walk with him.

To
GOD.
For His Highness.

Introduction

Take God's Hand and You Will Never Walk Alone.
Poems, Prayers and Promises—of Healing Peace, Love, Joy and Hope.
Encouraging words for living in the fullness of God's richest promises and blessings through his Love, Mercy and Grace.
Telling Poetry, alive with scripture to invigorate, and uplift, to bring Peace, Joy and Hope to all who live with Pain, Loneliness, Loss, Grief and Sadness.
Motivation for those who suffer Despair, Anxiety, Hopelessness.
For everyone who has ever felt forgotten, anyone who bears the scars and the weight of life in a world that at times seem very lonely, unkind and uncaring. God has not forgotten you.
The accompanying scriptures of his promises reach out to those about to give up on Life, Love, and Tomorrow, restoring Faith, Happiness and Joy for living in God's Peace.
A spiritual, realistic reinforcement of God's Love through his words, right out of the Bible. His Scriptural Promises.
Start living life again to the fullest in God's Truth, Word and Way as you take the Lord's hand and walk with him through life.
God is with us always– he loves us and he cares for us. He promises never to leave or forsake us. He wants us to be happy and live in Peace and Joyful Obedience, putting all our cares and trust in him always.
God loves us like no one can ever love us and he loves us much more than we can ever know. His love is unfathomable.
The words of each poem mirror the words of the accompanying scripture– interwoven to flow together as Poems, Prayers and Promises.
Start the journey now.
Take God's Hand and You Will Never Walk Alone.

God Loves You

I know you feel lonely, and at times you are so very sad,
I wish there was something I could do to make your heart feel glad.
I know you miss your loved ones—dear souls that have gone before,
And how I wish you would just smile and let your spirit soar.
Sometimes you feel depressed, and when you hurt, you cry,
It really, truly breaks my heart when you say you want to die.
There are times when you feel let down, by the ones you love the most.
When your heartfelt love goes unseen, that's when it hurts the worst.
I know your life has not been all roses, you've been through the mill,
And at times it seems as though the journey is still uphill.
What I love the most about you, and this I know for sure,
Is that you believe and trust in God and strive to live within his law.
I know that you are human and your tender heart feels pain,
And as you search for peace and joy, I will repeat what God says again,
Our Father God—he loves us, he loves us oh so much,
And whenever you feel lonely, reach out and feel his healing touch.
You are a precious child to him, find rest in his loving arms.
Trust and believe, have faith in God, he can make a raging ocean calm,
For he is God, our maker and yes, he knows your pain,
He knows everything about you, he calls you by your name.
God made you with a spirit of joy, for Victory, through His Might,
He will give you courage, you have already WON this fight.
So please cast away your sadness, stem the flow of tears,
Trust in the Lord to lift you up and take away your fears.
God is always close to you—he cares for and loves you,
When you kneel down to pray tonight, just smile and say—Thank you.
I love you too.

John 14:27 KJV

Peace I leave with you, my peace I give unto you, not as the world giveth, I give unto you. Let not your heart be troubled, neither let it be afraid.

Luke 6:21 NIV

Blessed are you who hunger now, for you will be satisfied.
Blessed are you who weep now, for you will laugh.

Joshua 1:5 ESV

No man shall be able to stand before you all the days of your life.
Just as I was with Moses, so I will be with you.
I will not leave you or forsake you.

John 3:16 NIV

For God so loved the world that he gave his one and only Son,
that whoever believes in him shall not perish but have eternal life.

"No matter what storm you face, you need to know that God loves you. He has not abandoned you."

—Rev. Franklin Graham

For Mother Helen.

—Stokesdale, NC— USA

Life's Pathway is Not a Road Race

On Earth's road to Heaven, it is easy to lose our way,
Some of us fall down, some stall in our tracks—
Others, lost in dark alleys, will forever stay.
But we should remember and keep in mind,
As we forge our paths and seek to find,
A life's journey is not always a swift road race,
So, keep going, no matter—whatever your pace.
If you fall, get back up, stay on the course,
Remember, God is your strength, he is the source.
For sure we will stumble and we will slip,
And at life's crossroads we may get tripped.
Yet despite the hurdles, we cannot stop,
We must seek to find the spiritual top.
The main goal is to stay the course,
Living focused on God's guiding light,
Knowing that from here on; to eternity,
God is with us, in all of his might.

Ecclesiastes 9:11 NIV

I have seen something else under the sun, the race is not to the swift or the battle to the strong, nor does food come to the wise or wealth to the brilliant or favor to the learned, but time and chance happen to them all.

Psalm 119:105 KJV

Thy word is a lamp unto my feet and a light unto my path.

Hebrews 12:1 ESV

Therefore, since we are surrounded by so great a cloud of witnesses, let us also lay aside every weight, and sin which clings so closely, and let us run with endurance the race that is set before us.

Psalm 16:11 ESV

You make known to me the path of life; in your presence there is fullness of joy, at your right hand are pleasures forevermore.

"Wisely and slow—they stumble that run fast."
—William Shakespeare

Breath of Hope and Life

As long as we have breath in us, we possess life's light,
Spiritual fires that once burned deep within, can surely reignite,
But at this moment, our life's force seems so diminished,
Once raging spiritual fires now almost extinguished.
Waning breath, still keeps embers of hope glowing,
This warm force of life is what keeps hope flowing.
We must hold on to hope, kindle the still flickering flame,
While we exist; have breath in us, life we must reclaim.
Have hope in the Lord, keep trusting, knowing,
Surely, soon we will feel our spirit's fire growing.
Call on the Lord, before him we should kneel,
All wounded souls that bow to ask, he will surely heal.
Draw in deeply, breathe the full breath of life again,
Seize your life, it's God's free gift to you my friend.
Keep reaching, praying, to yourself always be true,
God's spirit is right here, right now, alive and well in you.
Breathe in Life—The Holy Spirit.

Psalm 150:6 KJV

Let everything that hath breath praise the Lord.

Psalm 31:24 KJV

Be of good courage and he shall strengthen your heart,
all ye that hope in the Lord.

Job 12:10 KJV

In whose hands is the soul of every living thing and the breath of all mankind.

Job 33:4 NIV

The spirit of God has made me; the breath of the almighty gives me life.

"The breath of life is divine grace of God."
—Lailah Gifty Akita

Another Blessed Day

Some days you awake, feeling sad, all alone,
So tired, discouraged, you just want to go home.
Don't despair, just know this—you have already won this fight,
For God is in control, he's in your corner, in all his awesome might.
Remember; there is no one greater than God, who is life,
So, on dark dismal days let that knowledge suffice.
Thank God for the breath that he gives you today,
Know deep in your heart, he is with you always.
Ask him to restore you and truly believe,
For that's a sure promise for you to receive.
Keep faith in God when dark clouds blow in,
Draw strength from his spirit, for he lives within.
Keep Faith, Trust God, Spring Hope as bright as the sun,
And believe in your heart that this battle is won!

Isaiah 40:31 KJV

But they that wait upon the Lord shall renew their strength,
they shall mount up with wings like eagles, they shall run
and not be weary and they shall walk and not faint.

Jeremiah 1:19 NLT

They will fight you, but they will fail. For I am with you,
and I will take care of you. I, the Lord, have spoken.

2 Chronicles 20:17 ESV

You will not need to fight in this battle. Stand firm, hold your position, and see the salvation of the Lord on your behalf,
O Judah and Jerusalem. Do not be afraid and do not be dismayed. Tomorrow go out against them, and the Lord will be with you.

Psalm 146:5 KJV

Happy is he that hath the God of Jacob for his help, whose hope is in the Lord his God

"Let us then, be up and doing, with a heart for any fate–
Still achieving, still pursuing, learn to labor and to wait."

—Henry Wadsworth Longfellow

Arise and Reach Out to Jesus

God blessed you again with another day,
When you got out of bed today.
And yes, the day seems so sad—you dread,
You'd rather sulk and stay in bed.
Do get up, and look at life today,
See sun, see clouds, feel rain.
The Lord who made this very day,
Our God—He knows your pain.
And tomorrow's hope may come with fear,
Yes; sadness, gloom, they all lurk near.
We have to pray and ask the Lord,
To remove our doubts and fears;
And when we pray, we must believe,
God knows our fears, and hears our prayers.
Ask him for strength and courage,
Pray for peace and joy to face the coming days.
Be strong, hold fast in faith—believing,
He will lead you through the storms always.

Joshua 1:9 NLT

This is my command; be strong and courageous!
Do not be afraid or discouraged. For the Lord your
God is with you wherever you go."

Psalm 31:24 NLT

So be strong and courageous, all you who put your hope in the Lord.

Proverbs 3:6 KJV

In all thy ways acknowledge him and he shall direct thy paths.

Psalm 145:19 ESV

He fulfills the desire of those who fear him, he also hears their cry and saves them.

Psalm 92:2 KJV

To shew forth thy lovingkindness in the morning and thy faithfulness every night.

"When you arise in the morning, think of what a precious privilege it is to be alive, to breathe, to think, to enjoy, to love."
—Marcus Aurelius

You are with Me Always

Emmanuel

I thank you Lord for your breath of life—my soul,
Thanks for your blessings, mercy, favor; untold.
When I am anxious or lonely and feel lost in the rush,
I know I can reach out and feel your comforting touch.
It is your love only, that keeps me up in this world,
Your peace, joy and courage, all your mercies unfold.
Thanks for caring for me in a world that's gone wild,
I am at peace Father, just knowing, I am your child.
Abide in me Lord and lead me always, I pray,
To live in your light for the rest of my days.

Matthew 28:20 NLT

Teach these new disciples to obey all the commands
I have given you. And be sure of this; I am with you always,
even to the end of the age.

1 Thessalonians 5:5 KJV

Ye are all the children of light and the children of the day,
we are not of the night nor of darkness.

Psalm 28:7 ESV

The Lord is my strength and my shield; in him my heart trusts, and I am helped, my heart exults, and with my song I give thanks to him.

"The best of all, is God with us."
—John Wesley

Reach for God's Perfection

How would we learn to rise up, if we did not fall?
And how would we know to press forward,
If our backs were not up against a wall?
We would never build true faith, if we could not let go,
It is how we learn to live, that's how spiritual perfection grows.
For we would never realize, we could rise up to stand tall,
If we never tripped or stumbled or slipped and took a fall.
We learn from our experiences, from the good and bad,
That's how we foster wisdom, thru the sad days and the glad.
Yes, life will bring us challenges and sometimes walls start closing in,
It's when we draw on God's strength; our spiritual power begins.
We must live to face each moment, a minute, a day, a year,
Always relying on God our father, trusting, knowing he is always near.
So, whenever you stumble on the road, through God's space and time,
Get up and keep on moving, reaching; keeping all this in mind.
For If we did not ever stumble, or when reaching, slip or fall,
We would never crest life's summit or ever stand so tall.

Psalm 37:24 KJV

Though he fall, he shall not be utterly cast down,
for the Lord upholdeth him with his hand.

Psalm 145:14 NLT

The Lord helps the fallen and lifts those bent beneath their loads.

Deuteronomy 4:29 ESV

But from there you will seek the Lord your God and you will find him, if you search after him with all your heart and with all your soul.

Micah 7:8 KJV

Rejoice not against me, O mine enemy; when I fall, I shall arise, when I sit in darkness, the Lord shall be a light unto me.

"Every calamity is to be overcome by endurance."

—Virgil

Cheer Up and Let God Lighten your Burdens

In days gone by, when life's woes became impossible to bear,
Angels appeared to folk, proclaiming, "fear not, be of good cheer."
Now if we are to experience abundant life, joy in God's "Good Cheer,"
We must first release our burdens into his almighty care.
Yet today, alone we struggle, carrying all life's heavy weight,
Instead of cutting loose the load and relying on God with faith.
We should fully trust in the Lord, relying on his strength and love,
Remember the promises made to us by our Father above.
The Lord is the one who says this the best,
"Come all ye heavy laden and I will give you rest. "
Call on his strength now, let your tired heart be renewed,
And watch as the dark skies of life turn placidly blue.
Give him all your burdens, release to him your fears,
Start living life in Peace and Joy, in God's promise of Good Cheer.

Matthew 11:28 ESV

Come unto me all who labor and are heavy laden
and I will give you rest.

Psalm 55:22 NLT

Give your burdens to the Lord, and he will take care of you.
He will not permit the godly to slip and fall.

Nehemiah 8:10 KJV

Go your way, eat the fat and drink the sweet and send
portions unto them for whom nothing is prepared,
for this day is holy unto our Lord, neither be sorry,
for the joy of the Lord is your strength.

John 15:33 KJV

These things I have spoken unto you, that in me ye might have peace.
In the world ye shall have tribulation, but be of good cheer;
I have overcome the world.

"Just as Christian came up to the Cross, his burden loosed from off his shoulders, fell from off his back, and began to tumble down the hill, and so it continued to do till it came to the mouth of the sepulcher. There it fell in, and I saw it no more!"

—John Bunyan

Do Not Give Up—Stay the Course

When you're down and feeling lonely, discouragement creeps in,
Do not give up, stay on the course, draw strength from God within.
Loneliness is an ancient, dark illusion that's been used to make us sad,
When for life we should be grateful and for breath we should be glad.
Start right now—shake off your sadness, cast away your fears,
Do believe in this changing world, there is someone who cares.
You must believe and trust in God, always keep him in your sight,
Be sure to live a Godly life, try your best to do what's right.
Speak to the Lord in all you do, release all your cares and fears,
There is none better in this whole wide world to stop your every tear.
So, cheer up friend, know in your heart—you are not alone today,
Take the Heavenly Father's hand in hope, walk with him all the way.
Live Life to The Max!

Psalm 50:15 NIV

And call upon me in the day of trouble,
I will deliver thee and you will honor me.

Psalm 25:16 ESV

Turn to me and be gracious to me for I am lonely
and afflicted.

Romans 8:24—25 KJV

For we are saved by hope, but hope that is seen is not hope, for what a man seeth, why doth he yet hope for? But if we hope for that we see not, then do we with patience wait for it.

2 Corinthians 6:4 NIV

Rather, as servants of God we commend ourselves in every way, in great endurance; in troubles, hardships and distresses;

"Blessed is the one who perseveres under trial because, having stood the test, that person will receive the crown of life that the Lord has promised to those who love him."

—JAMES—THE BROTHER OF JESUS.

Take Control Lord—Lead Me

Father I ask you to lead me today,
Direct my life fully with each blessed new day.
Help me to slow down when am moving too fast,
To glean wisdom from victories and failures of my past.
Put the brakes on my tongue when it outruns my brain,
Help me stay focused— peace, patience—sustain.
Whenever I get flustered, Father, please settle me down,
Remind me O Lord of your calm presence all around.
And when fear and turmoil try to tear at my soul,
Grant me the wisdom to know you're in control.
To you I give all praise, the glory and honor,
Lord, bless and lead me always by your almighty power.

Psalm 23:3 KJV

He restoreth my soul, he leadeth me in the paths of righteousness for his name sake.

Job 33:33 NLT

But If not, then listen to me, keep silent
and I will teach you wisdom.

Psalm 143:10 KJV

Teach me to do thy will, for thou art my God, thy spirit is good, lead me into the land of uprightness.

Romans 8:14 ESV

For all who are led by the Spirit of God, are sons of God.

Isaiah 58:11 KJV

And the Lord shall guide thee continually
and satisfy thy soul in drought and make fat
thy bones and thou shalt be like a watered
garden and like a spring of water,
whose waters fail not.

"When you accept the fact that sometimes seasons are dry and times are hard and that God is in control of both, you will discover a sense of divine refuge, because the hope then is in God and not in yourself."

—Charles R. Swindoll

God Calling Earth—God to Earth —Come in Earth

Read your Bible

Deafened by life's noisy clatter, as our busy world spins around;
We never hear God calling us, nor do we listen for his sound.
We get lost in our life's whirlpools; just trying to stay afloat,
And in the course that life's sun sets, most of us just miss the boat.
Yet in this worldly clatter, our Lord is very present here,
His Angels here among us too, God Omnipotent—he is everywhere.
And as we work and live our lives, trudging through the strife,
Take the time to reap God's treasures, when you read his words of life.
Keep looking, listening for him today, he is always very near,
And when we speak to God in truth—trust that he will surely hear.
Seek out his calling always, with patience, listen—do your part,
The one sure way to hear his sweet voice is to listen with your heart.

Revelation 3:20 ESV

Behold I stand at the door and knock,
if anyone hears my voice and opens the door,
I will come in to him and eat with him and he with me.

John 10:3 KJV

To him the porter openeth, and the sheep hear his voice; and he calleth his own sheep by name, and leadeth them out.

2 Peter 1:3 ESV

His divine power has granted to us all things that pertain to life and Godliness, through the knowledge of him who called us to his own glory and goodness.

2 Thessalonians 2:14 NLT

He called you to salvation when we told you the good news; now you can share in the glory of our Lord Jesus Christ.

"I was living an extremely burdensome life,
because each time I prayed, I became more clearly
aware of my faults. On one hand, God was calling me.
On the other, I was following the way of the world.
Doing what God wanted made me happy,
but I felt bound by the things of this world."

—SAINT TERESA OF AVILA

More Life Forevermore—A Prayer

Lord, we ask for direction in making the right choice,
Help us to be humble, so we can hear your guiding voice.
We thank you Lord Jesus, for every blessed new day,
Walk and talk with us always, along life's busy way.
Whenever we feel anxious and want to have our own way,
Give us patience Heavenly Father, keep us still I pray.
And should we choose a path in life, you do not intend to be,
Touch our hearts, our eyes, our souls; spiritually guide and let us see.
Thank you for hearing all our prayers, for opening and closing doors,
That lead to abundant peace with joy, more life- forever more.

John 10:10 KJV

The thief cometh not, but for to steal and to destroy,
I am come that they might have life and that they
might have it more abundantly.

John 5:24 ESV

Truly, truly, I say to you, whoever hears my word and believes him
who sent me has eternal life. He does not come into judgment,
but has passed from death to life.

2 Corinthians 9:8 NIV

And God is able to bless you abundantly, so that in all things at all times,
having all that you need, you will abound in every good work.

Isaiah 61:7 NIV

Instead of their shame, my people will receive a double portion and instead of disgrace, you will rejoice in your inheritance. And so, you will inherit a double portion in your land and everlasting joy will be yours.

"Expect your every need to be met.
Expect the answer to every problem.
Expect abundance on every level."
—Eileen Caddy

Redial God—Do not Hang Up on life.

When our troubles overshadow life and dark clouds drown blue sky,
In our fragile human state, we grow weak, we fear; some choose to die.
This is the time to stand firm, stay strong, weathering a new life storm,
For throughout our earthly existence, these "giants" of life will always form.
Some say God made the mountains, so we could learn to climb,
We must keep hope's lamplight shining through the dark of space and time.
And simply—this is how we grow strong—by knowing God is Always there,
And he will take all of your troubles, if in him you trust and fear.
God is with us everywhere, on the mountain tops, the bottom of the seas;
He is right beside you now—in the wind rustling through the trees.
Hey friend look up at the rainbow too, there is a promise he made to you,
Let your knees do all the dialing now and return God's call to you.
Do not hang up on God and life; hit redial—just make the call!
Believe and place your trust in Him, his love will never let you fall.
For this too shall pass

Romans 10:13 KJV

For whosoever shall call upon the name of the Lord shall be saved.

Psalm 91:15 KJV

He shall call upon me and I will answer him, I will be with him in trouble, I will deliver him and honor him.

Psalm 139: 8—10 KJV

If I ascend up in heaven, thou art there, if I make my bed in hell behold thou art there,
If I take the wings of the morning and dwell in the uttermost parts of the sea; Even there shall thy hand lead me and thy right hand shall hold me.

Job 33: 28 KJV

He will deliver his soul from going down into the pit and his life shall see the light.

Psalm 50:15 ESV

And call upon me in the day of trouble, I will deliver you,
and you shall glorify me.

"Fall seven times, stand up eight"

—Japanese Proverb

My Rock—My All—Forever

O Father, forever walk with me.
Lord, catch me when I fall.
You are my rock, my pillar of strength,
Your love, your grace, your All.
And If I did not have you Lord,
I would feel so hopeless in this place.
For your mercy—you God—I praise,
Am blessed to live within your grace.
I thank you for your loving care,
For countless blessings year to year.
I pray you will always live in me,
From today—into eternity.

2 Samuel 22:3 KJV

The God of my rock, in him will I trust, he is my shield and
the horn of my salvation, my high tower and my refuge,
my savior thou savest me from violence.

Psalm 62:7 ESV

On God rests my salvation and my glory;
my mighty rock, my refuge is God.

Isaiah 26:4 NIV

Trust in the Lord forever, for the Lord, the Lord himself,
is the Rock eternal.

Psalm 118:14 KJV

The Lord is my strength and song, and is become my salvation.

"The strength of a man consists in finding out the way in which God is going and going in that way too."
—Henry Ward Beecher

Lead Me Everyday

Father in heaven, I ask for guidance today,
Walk with me Jesus, lead me all the way.
Show and direct me, bless me always I pray.
Send angels to lead me with every new day.
I pray for existence in your mercy and grace,
Give me strength and wisdom to complete this race.
Keep me from danger and shield me from ill,
Correct and always lead me to do your will.
Lord Jesus, gentle shepherd, guide me on your path,
Keep me from straying, keep me from wrath.
Father, show me the road that I must walk through,
To find sweet rest and comfort that comes only from you.

Isaiah 49:10 KJV

They shall not hunger nor thirst, neither shall the heat nor the sun smite them, for he that hath mercy on them shall lead them, even by the springs of water shall he guide them.

Isaiah 48:17 NLT

This is what the Lord says; your Redeemer, the Holy One of Israel. "I am the Lord your God, who teaches you what is good for you and leads you along the paths you should follow."

Psalm 16:11 KJV

Thou wilt shew me the path of life, in thy presence is fullness of joy, at thy right hand there are pleasures forevermore.

Isaiah 30:21 KJV

And thine ears shall hear a word behind thee, saying, This is the way, walk ye in it, when ye turn to the right hand, and when ye turn to the left.

"Having thus chosen our course, without guile and with pure purpose, let us renew our trust in God, and go forward without fear and with manly hearts."

—Abraham Lincoln

The Godsent Touch of Love—Pass it On

There are seasons in life when our spirits are down,
And the simplest pleasures of fellowship cannot be found.
Those times in our lives when we do not ask, or want much;
They are just the moments we need a God sent Spiritual Touch.
For we all need love, fellowship; caring, human devotion,
Love gifts of creation, that are borne through emotion.
What does a hug cost, or a kiss, a smiling face?
How difficult is it to hug a heart, to warmly embrace?
Can you fathom the power of action, the love it can send?
Did you ever imagine, a broken heart you could mend?
A smile can say I love you and I care,
Come let me embrace you, hold you near.
Our love can say yes, you've got a friend,
Let's walk through that mile, get past this dark bend.
Compassion heals the heart's pain, love frees the Human Race,
Yes, that gentle touch, pat on the back, can put a smile on a sad face.
Sharing love is so filled with life, it holds an awesome power,
It can deliver a miraculous healing touch at the eleventh hour.
Do not hold back that God Sent Touch of Love today—
It is a blessing to share, you must give it away.
Use it openly, freely, to brighten someone's day.
Touching hearts with God's love, along life's busy way.

John 13:34—35 NIV

A new command I give you; Love one another. As I have loved you,
so, you must love one another.
By this everyone will know that you are my disciples, if you love one another.

Ephesians 4:32 KJV

And be kind one to another, tenderhearted, forgiving one another, even as God for Christ's sake has forgiven you.

1 Peter 5:14 KJV

Greet ye one another with a kiss of charity,
Peace be with you all that are in Christ. Amen.

Colossians 3:12 & 14 ESV

Put on then, as God's chosen ones, holy and beloved, compassionate hearts, kindness, humility, meekness, and patience, And above all these put on love, which binds everything together in perfect harmony.

"You cannot do a kindness too soon, for you never know how soon it will be too late."

—Ralph Waldo Emerson

The Ultimate Best Friend Forever

Our Eternal Lord

There are seasons in life when we walk alone;
On those days we may feel lonely and blue,
Then God sends someone down that very same road;
A friend, to walk those blue miles with you.
This undoubtedly is a friend God has placed in your way;
To share blessed moments along life's thruway,
A blessing to make the journey light and bright,
Adding shared joy and cheer to each day.
Yes, this time is Godsent, having friends so dear,
The pain and joy, this bond they share.
Then comes a new season in our lives one day;
When a dear friend may have to leave—fly away.
And on the days when you sit alone and reminisce;
all the faded, lost friendships, please remember this—
For it is a comforting truth you should know,
Throughout life, friends will always come and go.
Only God's fellowship is eternal, his love knows no end,
For he is the one and only Ultimate Forever Friend.
So, whenever you feel alone or just a little sad,
Remember this joyous truth and with a grateful heart be glad.
God will never abandon you, nor will he ever break your heart,
He's been with you always—together—forever—right from the very start.
Keep him close

Deuteronomy 31:8 NIV

The Lord himself goes before you and will be with you; he will never leave you nor forsake you. Do not be afraid, do not be discouraged.

Psalm 136:1 KJV

O give thanks unto the Lord for he is good and his mercies endureth forever.

Matthew 28:20 KJV

Teaching them to observe all things whatsoever I have commanded you and lo, I am with you always, even to the end of the world.

1 Corinthians 1:9 NLT

God will do this, for he is faithful to do what he says, and he has invited you into partnership with his Son, Jesus Christ our Lord.

"Every friendship with God and every love between Him and a soul is the only one of its kind."

—Janet Erskine Stuart

You are Never Alone—With Christ

Sometimes we are discouraged, life's woes, too much to bear,
Not believing our God is with us, we live life in constant fear.
Sadly, thinking we are alone, we live with heavy, lonely hearts,
Sorrow threatens to destroy us and rip our world apart.
Just when you think life is hopeless, you can bear the hurt no more,
Well; should your tears start flowing freely, let your knees drop to the floor.
Go on, cry out to Jesus, believe it—he is right there,
His love will never let you carry more than you can ever bear.
Why must we suffer trials—to reach out—find God—what do you suppose?
Only God has the true answer, he is the only one who knows.
Always trust God with all your heart, your life, your very soul,
And he will give you in return, peace, joy, love—in this his world.
When pain and anguish threaten—and you pray, trusting God will hear,
Remember, God listens to all his children and he will forever care.

Romans 10:13 KJV

For whosoever shall call upon the name of the Lord shall be saved.

Isaiah 4:6 NIV

It will be a shelter and shade from the heat of the day,
and a refuge and hiding place from the storm and rain.

Nahum 1:7 KJV

The Lord is good, a stronghold in the day of trouble;
and he knoweth them that trust him.

Take God's Hand and You Will Never Walk Alone

Psalm 91:1—5 NIV

Whoever dwells in the shelter of the Most High will rest
in the shadow of the Almighty.
I will say of the Lord "He is my refuge and my fortress,
my God, in whom I trust."
Surely, he will save you from the fowler's snare and from
the deadly pestilence.
He will cover you with his feathers and under his wings you
will find refuge; his faithfulness will be your shield and rampart.
You will not fear the terror of the night, nor the arrow that flies by day."

"And know that I am with you always; yes, to the end of time."

—Jesus Christ of Nazareth

Let Go of the Past

Do not Worry about Tomorrow— Keep on living Today

Choices made along life's way, may come back to hurt one day,
That's when we give our pain to God and let him lead the way.
For none of us are perfect and the future we do not know,
God uses our mistakes to give wisdom; experience for us to grow.
So, if a very precious loved one, may have seemed to go astray,
Or a soulmate may have grown apart from us, in an unexpected way;
Even when our plans for life do not turn out the way we want them to,
Remember, this is not the end; God said he has good plans in store for you.
Do not worry about tomorrow, live today and don't be sad,
For while we live, we learn to accept, life comes with good and bad.
We should reflect and realize, in this course that life is run,
We do not always have control in life's battles—lost or won.
The sages say that only time will make the crooked straight,
Today we have to keep on living, keep holding on to hope with faith.
So, let go the hurt, release the pain—pray—trust God to lead the way,
Give him the past, let him have tomorrow, find strength in him today.

Matthew 6:34 KJV

Take therefore no thought for the morrow,
for the morrow shall take thought for the things of itself,
sufficient unto the day is the evil thereof.

Jeremiah 31:13 ESV

Then shall the maidens rejoice in the dance and the young men and the old men shall be merry, I will turn their mourning into joy. I will comfort them and give them gladness for sorrow.

Isaiah 43:18 NIV

Forget the former things; do not dwell on the past.

Jeremiah 29:11 NIV

For I know the plans I have for you, declares the Lord, a plan to prosper you and not to harm you, plans to give you a hope and a future.

"Even though you may want to move forward in your life, you may have one foot on the brakes. In order to be free, we must learn how to let go. Release the hurt. Release the fear. Refuse to entertain your old pain.
The energy it takes to hang onto the past is holding you back from a new life. What is it you would let go of today?"

—Mary Manin Morrissey

A Prayer to Stand Tall for Jesus

Jesus, my Lord; today I really need your touch,
My spiritual life does not amount to much.
Grant me peace and courage to obey your call,
Gird me with wisdom and truth to stand above it all.
Strengthen me with your armor to do your will,
Pray, keep me from evil and shield me from ill.
And if I should slip and go astray,
I ask you Lord, with me please stay.
Live in me always and make me strong,
Lord, talk with me as we walk along.
Lead and keep me by grace every day,
Shine your lovelight to show me Heaven's way.
Father, please lift me up if I should fall,
One day soon, I will stand tall—
For you Lord.

Luke 21:36 KJV

Watch therefore and pray always that ye may be accounted worthy to escape all these things that shall come to pass and to stand before the son of man.

1 Chronicles 23:30 ESV

And they were to stand every morning thanking and praising the Lord and likewise at evening.

Ephesians 6:13 ESV

Therefore, take up the whole armor of God, that you may be able to withstand in the evil day, and having done all, to stand firm.

Psalm 73:26 NIV

My flesh and my heart may fail, but God is the strength of my heart and my portion forever.

"Never think that you can live to God by your own power or strength, but always look to and rely on him for assistance, yea, for all strength and grace."

—David Brainard

Amazing Grace IOU— Endless Love

I owe my life to Christ—crucified—a sacrifice payed for me,
I will forever praise and thank him, worship him on bended knee.
Yes, I will lift my voice in love, sing praises to my father above,
I will exalt his name forever, thank him for his endless love.
I asked, "Father, how can I repay you, for your awesome love for me?"
The answer came back through his word— "my child it's all for free"
Again, I asked the father, "how could such endless love be free to me?"
His word said "all I ask of you my child, is that you love me endlessly."

Matthew 22:37—38 NLT

Jesus replied, you must love the Lord thy God with
all your heart all your soul and all your mind.
This is the first and greatest commandment.

Romans 6:23 NIV

For the wages of sin is death, but the free gift of God is eternal
life through Christ Jesus our Lord.

John 15:13—14 KJV

Greater love hath no man than this, that a man lay
down his life for a friend. Ye are my friends,
if ye do whatsoever I command you.

John 1:16 ESV

For from his fullness we have all received, grace upon grace.

Psalm 146:1—2 NLT

Praise the Lord!
Let all that I am praise the Lord.
I will praise the Lord as long as I live.
I will sing praises to my God with my dying breath

"I firmly believe that in every situation, no matter how difficult,
God extends grace greater than the hardship, and strength and peace of mind that can lead us to a place higher than where we were before."

—Andy Griffith

My Day Your Way

As I awoke from sleep today,
I thanked the Lord for another day.
A brand, new day, I feel the thrill,
Another day to do God's will.
Lord, how can I serve you today?
Show me please Father, show me your way.
Keep and guide me throughout this day.
Sustain and lead me please, I pray.
And my soul tonight, God; bless and keep,
As I lay at your feet in sweet, restful sleep.

Psalm 25:5 KJV

Lead me in thy truth and teach me, for thou art the God of my salvation, on thee do I wait all the day long.

Psalm 5:3 NIV

In the morning Lord, you hear my voice; in the morning I lay my requests before you and wait expectantly.

Psalm 143:8 ESV

Let me hear in the morning of your steadfast love, for in you I trust. Make me know the way I should go, for to you I lift up my soul.

Psalm 119:175 NIV

Let me live that I may praise you, and may your laws sustain me.

"To live in the light of a new day and an unimaginable and unpredictable future, you must become fully present to a deeper truth—not a truth from your head, but a truth from your heart—not a truth from your ego, but a truth from the highest source."

—Debbie Ford

Spiritual Friend—Heaven Sent

It never ceases to amaze me, how God knows what we need most,
And everything he sends our way, overflows with infinite love.
For a season the road may get lonely, the horizon looks like a dead end,
That's when our Father, in his grace, may send a brand, new friend.
A kindred soul to walk with us, through those barren, cold, dark days.
A friend that actually prays with us, as we seek to find our way.
A heaven—sent friend is the rare soul, who really truly cares,
Someone who feels your joys and pains and may even share a tear.
When our Lord sends such a kindred spirit, sharing love and pain,
Keep in mind as time moves on, this love we must sustain.
To each other stay always true, be sure to say "friend I love you,"
For friends who share a bond so deep, blessed from heaven above,
Will come to realize in time, it is God's gift wrapped up in love.

1 Peter 1:22 ESV

Having purified your souls by your obedience to the truth for a sincere brotherly love, love one another earnestly from a pure heart.

Hebrews 13:1 ESV

Let brotherly love continue.

Proverbs 17:17 NLT

A friend is always loyal, and a brother is born to help in time of need.

2 Peter 1:7 KJV

And to Godliness, brotherly kindness and to brotherly kindness, charity.

Proverbs 27:9 KJV

Ointment and perfume rejoice the heart, so doth the sweetness of a man's friend by hearty counsel.

"A real friend is one who walks in
when the rest of the world walks out."
—Walter Winchell

For Ron, Kersten, Samuel and Zach
—Greensboro, NC –USA

Keep Me from Temptation

My Lord, I try my very best each day,
To live my life just as you say,
But there are times when I just fall back,
The resistance against sin, I seem to lack.
And though I try my best to follow in your way,
There just always comes another trying day.
And with each passing, living hour,
I urgently need your spiritual power.
Keep me from temptation and forgive me I pray,
Strengthen and uplift me to trust and obey.
Deliver me from evil, wash me in your blood,
I only want to please YOU— to honor you my God.

James 4:7 NIV

Submit yourselves, then, to God, resist the devil
and he will flee from you.

Matthew 26:41 KJV

Watch and pray that ye enter not into temptation,
The spirit indeed is willing but the flesh is weak.

Galatians 5:17 ESV

For the desires of the flesh are against the Spirit, and the
desires of the Spirit are against the flesh, for these are opposed
to each other, to keep you from doing the things you want to do.

Luke 11:4 ESV

And forgive us our sins, for we ourselves forgive everyone who is indebted to us. And lead us not into temptation.

"We are too apt to forget that temptation to sin will rarely present itself to us in its true colors, saying, "I am your deadly enemy, and I want to ruin you forever in hell." Oh no! Sin comes to us like Judas, with a kiss; like Joab, with outstretched hand and flattering words. The forbidden fruit seemed good and desirable to Eve; yet it cast her out of Eden. Walking idly on his palace roof seemed harmless enough to David; yet it ended in adultery and murder. Sin rarely seems (like) sin at first beginnings. Let us then watch and pray, lest we fall into temptation."

—JC Ryle

Let Life Heal and Grow Again

I was going to call you one of these days,
I would have called if I knew God would take you away.
I still want to say I am sorry, and I love you—
God knows, I would have called every day, if I knew.
It hurts me to think that I cannot see you for a while.
I feel the emptiness, loneliness; like an orphaned child.
I ask, "can the peace of forgiveness come back around?"
And today, no answers, just remorse can be found.
They say time the great healer comes with tomorrow,
And the love of God will heal regret and sorrow.
They say people living with grief, should know—
God's healing mercy through grace will flow—
And a healing peace will bloom and grow.
I ask God to take this pain of sadness away.
Pray his healing grace brings a brighter day.
I will remember the evergreen of our yesterdays.
I just wanted to tell you—I loved you always.

Matthew 5:4 NIV

Blessed are those who mourn for they will be comforted.

1 Peter 1:3 NIV

Praise be to the God and Father of our Lord Jesus Christ!
In his great mercy he has given us new birth into a living hope
through the resurrection of Jesus Christ from the dead,

Psalm 147:3 ESV

He heals the broken in heart and binds up their wounds.

John 14:18 KJV

I will not leave you comfortless, I will come to you.

"Your sorrow Itself shall be turned into Joy. Not the sorrow to be taken away and joy to be put in its place, but the very sorrow which now grieves you shall be turned into joy.
God not only takes away the bitterness and gives sweetness in its place, but turns the Bitterness into Sweetness itself."

—Charles Haddon Spurgeon

Arise and Walk with God

Come on, Wake Up, Get Up—Arise! thank the Lord for life.
Cast away the fear and gloom, unbind your heart from strife.
Today you are blessed with life, for you still breathe on planet Earth.
God has a good plan for you, formed in love, long before your birth.
Free yourself from bondage, ask God to break the chains,
If it's too dark to find your way, then let him take the reins.
Arise! reach out, keep on living, no matter how *ugh* you feel,
In this life of joy and pain believe God's love is for real.
So, come on, rise up, reach for God's hand and let him walk with you,
Walk in faith and take his hand, and he will lead you through.
Call on him now for joy and strength, ask him to take away your pain,
Believe from this very moment on, you will never walk alone again.
*Git up! *

Ephesians 5:14 KJV

Wherefore he saith, awake thou that sleepest, and arise from the dead and Christ shall give thee light.

Isaiah 60:1 ESV

Arise, shine, for your light has come, and the glory of the Lord has risen upon you.

Psalm 22:9 &11 KJV

But You are He who took me out of the womb; you made me trust while on my mother's breasts. Be not far from me, for trouble is near; for there is none to help.

Colossians 3:1 ESV

If then you have been raised with Christ, seek the things that are above, where Christ is, seated at the right hand of God.

"God is in the sadness and the laughter,
in the bitter and the sweet."

—Neale Donald Walsch

A Prayer of Thanks

For the Light of Love and Mercy

Oh, heavenly Father, my Lord above,
I thank you for your peace and love.
I praise you for your blessings over me,
For countless mercies, favor, free.
I thank you Lord for a meal to eat,
Clothes on my back and shoes on my feet.
Oh Father, thanks for health and strength,
For joy; courage to travel the journey's length.
Thanks for your love, its bright, comforting light,
That shines in, to warm my heart every day and night.
Keep it burning

Matthew 5:14 NLT

You are the light of the world, like a city on a hilltop that cannot be hidden.

John 9:5 ESV

As long as I am in the world, I am the light of the world.

Psalm 85:10 KJV

Mercy and truth are met together, righteousness and peace have kissed each other.

Joel 2:26 ESV

You shall eat in plenty and be satisfied, and praise the name of the Lord your God, who has dealt wondrously with you. And my people shall never again be put to shame.

"When you rise in the morning, give thanks for the light, for your life, for your strength. Give thanks for your food and for the joy of living. If you see no reason to give thanks, the fault lies with you."

—Tecumseh

The Spiritual Renewal of Life

Love Memories

The best days of our lives, when we reminisce,
Are the good times we spent sharing love's, tenderness.
When we are blessed to share mutual love by fate,
Precious time with a kindred spirit, is wonderful, so great.
Yet on every life's journey comes the time we must say goodbye,
And someday, from this earth, all living souls must fly.
We must accept this passage rite—renewal, resurrection from earth,
Celestial plan from dust and dirt—life's cycle to spiritual birth.
So today if you feel sad or all alone, a precious soulmate, spirit flown,
And if you truly have deeply loved; and to be loved, you know,
Then let the love heal the hurt and pain; never let the memories go.
For true love is eternal and forever lives within the soul,
This love can bridge the aching void across the spirit world.
Time's eternal, love memories will never let souls part,
Embrace God's grace of spiritual renewal and heal your broken heart.

Revelation 21:4 KJV

And God shall wipe away all tears from their eyes and there shall be no more death, neither sorrow nor crying, neither shall there be any more pain, for the former things are passed away.

Revelation 21:5 NIV

He who was seated on the throne said I am making
everything new! Then he said, write this down,
for these words are trustworthy and true.

1 John 5:11 ESV

And this is the testimony, that God gave us eternal life,
and this life is in his Son.

2 Corinthians 5:17 NLT

This means that anyone who belongs to Christ has become a new person.
The old life is gone; a new life has begun.

"Although it's difficult to see beyond the sorrow today,
Looking back in memory may help comfort you tomorrow."

—Author unknown

Sister to Sister—Our Loves Lives Forever

When I heard the sad news, I could not hold back the tears,
The sorrow and grief just took me back to yesteryears,
When we laughed and played as kids, not a care in the world,
Only us, two sisters in our own backyard world.
To think that I told you hello only yesterday,
Today I feel the sorrow of your going away.
In life's big picture we will always ask—why?
Sometimes the answers come, as life flows on by.
I thank God for the blessing of a sister like you,
To share laughter and tears, the best of our years.
But now I am saying goodbye and it's so hard to let go,
I try to stem the tears, yet they openly flow.
I ask God to comfort me through my pain,
Till the day when I meet you in heaven again.
So, for now my sister, I'll say our last earthly goodbyes,
And forever cherish our treasure, for true love never dies.

Luke 20:36 KJV

Neither can they die anymore, for they are equal
unto the angels and are the children of God,
being the children of the resurrection.

Psalm 49:15 NIV

But God will redeem me from the realm of the dead,
he will surely take me to himself,

John 16:22 NLT

So, you have sorrow now, but I will see you again;
then you will rejoice, and no one can rob you of that joy.

"Death has its revelations—the great sorrows which open
the heart opens the mind as well—light comes to us with
our grief. As for me, I have faith—I believe in a future life.
How could I do otherwise? My daughter was a soul;
I saw this soul. I touched it, so to speak."
—Victor Hugo.

For Jerri.
—FT Lauderdale. FL, USA

Feel the Fullness in His Care

When you feel weary and broken, just plain worn out,
And you envision tomorrow shrouded in doubt.
When your faith is weakened and you can find no rest,
Call on God to restore you, fill you up with his best.
Grasp the hope of salvation from God with great faith,
His deliverance comes to believers who hope and wait.
So, no matter how hopelessly lost you may feel,
Keep believing in God, he is our strength, our shield.
For sure he is our Rock Fortress, our Strong Tower,
Reach out to him now, live in his awesome power.
Keep anchored in faith as the storm batters and rages,
Do not let go, hold strong to the Rock of Ages.

Psalm 18:2 KJV

The Lord is my rock and fortress and my deliverer,
my God in whom I trust, my buckler and the horn
of my salvation and my high tower.

Matthew 24:13 ESV

But the one who endures to the end will be saved.

Psalm 29:11 NIV

The Lord gives strength to his people; the Lord blesses his people with peace.

Matthew 18:11 KJV

For the son of man is come to save that which was lost.

"The everlasting Father who cares for you today
will take care of you tomorrow, and every day.
Either he will shield you from suffering, or he will give
you unfailing strength to bear it"

—St. Francis de Sales

Goodbye Mortal Hello Angel

Joy in Heaven

A mortal journey is complete this day,
Safe in God's bosom, his beloved child;
Angels sang the welcome to the end of earth's last mile,
In paradise, cherubs celebrate with harps, trumpets and fife,
For there is great joy in heaven when a mortal finds eternal life.
Loved ones who live on this side of Heaven, yes, we will surely grieve,
But in God's time, grief will subside when in Heaven we believe.
So, live on in peace with treasured memories, let joy live in your heart,
Knowing we will meet again in heaven and never, ever have to be apart.
Weep for a while and then maybe, no more, let eternal love shine,
Believe we will all be together again someday—
All Angels, in God's Eternal Time.
Welcome Angel

Luke 15:10 KJV

Likewise, I say unto you, there is joy in the presence of
the angels of God over one sinner that repenteth.

Luke 23:43 NIV

Jesus answered him, Truly I tell you,
today you will be with me in paradise.

John 14:2—3 KJV

In my father's house are many mansions,
if it were not so I would have told you.
I go to prepare a place for you.
And if I go to prepare a place for you,
I will come and receive you unto myself,
that where I am, there ye will be also.

Psalm 37:37 KJV

Mark the perfect man and behold the upright,
for the end of that man is peace.

John 11:25—26 ESV

Jesus said to her, "I am the resurrection and the life.
Whoever believes in me, though he die, yet shall he live,
and everyone who lives and believes in me shall never die.
Do you believe this?"

"Our Lord has written the promise of resurrection,
not only in books alone, but in every leaf in springtime."

—MARTIN LUTHER

Do Your Best Always

If Jesus knows the trouble we see,
Then what are we so worried about?
All he asks us to do is to obey him, follow his laws—
Be honest, work hard, give praise, sing, shout!
So, keep living life trusting Jesus, joyfully doing his will,
When life's troubles roll in, he promised to pick up the bill.
Each day of your life, do the best you can do,
And God's Best will always come right back to you.

Galatians 6:9 NLT

So, let's not get tired of doing what is good. At just the right time we will reap a harvest of blessing if we don't give up.

Job 36:11 KJV

If they obey and serve him, they shall spend their days in prosperity and their years in pleasures.

Philippians 4:19 NLT

And this same God who takes care of me will supply all your needs from his glorious riches, which have been given to us in Christ Jesus.

Psalm 23:6 ESV

Surely goodness and mercy shall follow me all the days of my life and I shall dwell in the house of the Lord forever.

"Fear God and work hard."

—DAVID LIVINGSTONE

The Choice Test

Choose Him in ALL

Choosing to do the right thing, becomes a conflicting plight,
It seems so much easier to quit, step away from God's guiding light.
We must have faith, trusting God—courage to pass this life test,
To make the very perfect choice—choose God's way and ditch all the rest.
Yes, at times we all will waver, when we feel anxious, insecure—
We open up our souls to doubt, when we should slam shut that door.
It is through uncertain times that faith and trust are put to the test,
So, stand strong, firm in Jehovah Jireh, and receive the very best.
God takes care of his children, when they choose him over all,
Trust in him with all of your heart and he will give you His All.
*Can U handle it All? *

Luke 12:31 NLT

Seek the kingdom of God above all else and he will
give you everything you need.

Psalm 119:173 NLT

Give me a helping hand, for I have chosen to
follow your commandments.

Lamentations 3:25 KJV

The Lord is good unto them that wait for him,
to the soul that seeketh him.

Psalm 2:12—13 ESV

Who is the man who fears the Lord?
Him will he instruct in the way that he should choose.
His soul shall abide in well—being, and his offspring shall inherit the land.

"Nothing harms or destroys us but the wrong use of that liberty of choice which God has entrusted to us."

—WILLIAM LAW

Faith and Trust = Synergy

Whenever we feel troubled and afraid, uncertain of the road ahead,
When our days seem sad and lonely or our thoughts are full of dread,
Keep this in mind as you travel on, hold on to your *Faith*, don't give up!
We must *Trust* God as we press on, if we are to make it to our stop.
In the gloomy presence around us, our trust can never cease,
For if our hearts lack faith and trust, we will never find true peace.
Although we can't see faith and trust, they stand so very, very tall,
They are the pillars of our strength, when our backs are against the wall.
And when we climb on faith and trust be sure to hold on tight,
For as we rise up on the height of hope, we will see life in a new light.
The toughest task is to start the climb, to awaken from life's dark sleep.
True *Synergy* is thus defined, when Faith and Trust—they meet.
*Start the climb today—God's got the Ropes! *

Psalm 125:1 ESV

Those who Trust in the Lord are like Mount Zion,
which cannot be moved but abides forever.

Hebrews 11:1 NLT

Faith shows the reality of what we hope for; it is the
evidence of things we cannot see.

Hebrews 11:8 KJV

By Faith Abraham, when he was called to go out into a place which he should receive for an inheritance obeyed, and he went out not knowing wither he went.

Isaiah 12:2 NIV

Surely God is my salvation; I will trust and not be afraid. The Lord, the Lord himself, is my strength and my defense he has become my salvation.

"The whole is greater than the sum of its parts."

—Aristotle

Comfort Zone—
On the Narrow Holy Road

Life's mortal journey is chock full of bumps on the road,
At times, life itself feels like a very heavy load.
Yet still, we must live our lives acknowledging God's Grace,
Keeping faith and hope alive to endure our earthly race.
There are days we will falter and for a while lose sight,
But still we must stay focused, keep on doing what is right.
It is a constant struggle to stay on God's narrow holy road,
But the yoke becomes so easy if we ask Him to bear our load.
Trust God with your life's journey, in all matters, large or small,
Have faith he will always help you if you should ever fall.
For when we trust in the Lord and follow what he says,
He gives us peace and comfort by removing our fears.
So, keep trying to do as our Lord says we should,
Depart from sin and evil and always try to do good.
Forever give God the Glory and the Holy Praise,
Always in humility, with honor, voices thankfully raised.
Just knowing in our hearts, that Almighty God, first loved us,
Enables living in his comfort zone, in total faith and trust.

John 14:18 KJV

I will not leave you comfortless, I will come to you.

1 John 4:19 KJV

We love him, because he first loved us.

Psalm 23:4 KJV

Yea though I walk through the valley of the shadow
of death. I will fear no evil, for thou art with me,
thy rod and thy staff they comfort me.

Matthew 7:14 NIV

But small is the gate and narrow the road that leads to life,
and only a few find it.

Matthew 11:30 ESV

For my yoke is easy and my burden is light.

"The irony of the human condition is that it is the narrow
gate to life. Few find it because they are too fearful to look."

—Robert J Blizzard

A Forever God Season—In Perpetual Light

The dark, grey skies always turn to blue,
A timeless message of God's love for you.
A morning's dark has dawned so bright,
The cold earth warmed by God's awesome might.
Behold a cold, grey winter turn to green spring,
New life, rebirth and warmth God brings.
To change from dead grey to green; a tree,
A God blessed miraculous picture some just fail to see.
God sends his messages every day, all year,
Most of the time we never see nor hear.
This show of awesome power, illustrates his enduring love,
God keeps sending life messages in light from above;
Transmitting signs of hope, new life—his divine presence,
With color to brighten our way, to make the journey pleasant.
So, remember when the dark clouds of life change into light,
Or when grey clouds block out skies of blue,
Keep listening, looking at life's big live screen,
God is right there—always speaking to you.

Genesis 8:22 KJV

While the earth remaineth, seedtime and harvest,
and cold and heat, and summer and winter, and day
and night shall not cease.

Psalm 104:19 ESV

He made the moon to mark the seasons;
the sun knows it's time for setting.

Hebrews 13:8 NIV

Jesus Christ is the same yesterday, and today
and forever.

Mark 13:37 NLT

I say to you what I say to everyone; watch for him.

"Every moment of light and dark is a miracle."
—Walt Whitman

Jehovah Rapha has The Rx for Healing

It's difficult to describe the pain we are feeling,
We may need more than just a physical healing.
Burdened with life's woes, paralyzed with fears,
At times we are alone, worried, thinking nobody cares.
What we should know is, we hold the *Script—ure—*the cure,
Free access to the Master Physician—complete healing so pure.
Blessed to have the Anointed Physician always in the house,
A gift we should rise up, give thanks for, rejoice!
Trust him to free us from our bondage and pains,
Jehovah Rapha will heal us and break life's toxic chains.
When you ask him for help to remove your crippling fear,
You must fully release your burdens into his almighty care.
We should follow the Great Doctor's orders; it is a must,
Have Faith, Patience, and most of all—Trust.
Live in peace, believing he always hears our prayers,
Our Great Physician has the cure, to dry all our tears.
Open your heart and mind to this awesome light,
Feel the mastery of his supernatural, healing might.
Fill your heart with joy, trade in old sorrow,
Have faith now, today, bright hope for tomorrow.
Live in God's healing comfort throughout your years,
Always trusting, believing, Jehovah Rapha truly cares.

1 Peter 5:7 KJV

Casting all your care upon him, for he careth for you.

Jeremiah 30:17 NLT

I will give you back your health and heal your wounds, says the Lord. For you are called an outcast, Jerusalem for whom no one cares.

Luke 4:18 KJV

The spirit of the Lord is upon me because he hath anointed me to preach the Gospel to the poor, he hath sent me to heal the brokenhearted, to preach deliverance to the captives and recovering of sight to the blind, to set at liberty them that are bruised.

Malachi 4:2 ESV

But for you who fear my name, the sun of righteousness shall rise with healing in its wings. You shall go out leaping like calves from the stall.

Mark 2:17 KJV

When Jesus heard it, he saith unto them, they that are whole have no need of the Physician, but they that are sick. I came not to call the righteous, but the sinners to repentance.

Psalm 103:3 NLT

He forgives all my sins, and heals all my diseases.

* Jehovah Rapha—The God who heals *

"How sweet the name of Jesus sounds in a believer's ear!
It soothes his sorrows, heals his wounds and drives away his fear."

—JOHN NEWTON

Transcendent Love

I love you as a dear, close friend and have great respect for you,
And you say you love me too—shouldn't you revere our friendship too?
Not sure if this is kindred love that enjoins two souls by fate,
Or is it blind and lonely lust that opens forbidden, ancient gates?
Illicit love comes at too great a spiritual price—never would God Bless,
It is a great temptation of the flesh, an ancient, repeated human test.
Transcendent Love bonds souls with joy, endless love, eternal trust,
If and when this love comes, how will we know this is meant for us?
I pray the Lord will lead and guide us, as time keeps flowing by,
For sure within God's laws of life, we both must still abide.
Whatever God has destined for us, will surely come to be,
It's just like faith, we cannot see, so we must maintain spirituality.
And how do we get there? —I do not know, right now no answers come to me.
I am caught between the wrong and right, a moral conflict, a spiritual fight,
But while I search for answers true, I will live within God's sight,
For to ultimately embrace Transcendent Love,
I must live Holy in God's pure light.

Psalm 25:12 KJV

What man is he that feareth the Lord?
Him shall he teach in the way that he shall choose.

1 Corinthians 13:4—7 NIV

Love is patient, love is kind. It does not envy,
it does not boast, it is not proud.
It does not dishonor others, it is not self—seeking,
it is not easily angered—it keeps no record of wrongs.
Love does not delight in evil but rejoices with the truth.
It always protects, always trust, always hopes, always perseveres.

1 Corinthians 6:18—20 KJV

Flee fornication. Every sin that a man doeth is without the body,
but he that committeth fornication sinneth against his own body.
What? know ye not that your body is the temple of the Holy Ghost
which is in you, which ye have of God, and ye are not your own?
For ye are bought with a price; therefore, glorify God in your body,
and in your spirit, which are God's.

Ecclesiastes 12:13—14 NIV

Now all has been heard, here is the conclusion of the matter;
Fear God and keep his commandments, for this is the duty of all.
mankind. For God will bring every deed into judgment,
including every hidden thing, whether it is good or evil.

"This idea of the transcendent power of the Supreme Being is essentially connected with that by which the whole duty of man is summed up—obedience to His will."

—JOHN QUINCY ADAMS

Awesome Faith—Never Lose It

For the people holding on to faith—never, ever let go,
To souls who on the Lord await, his grace will always show.
In life our faith is tested, through sunshine, through hard rain,
Throughout our lives we learn to accept all life's joy and pain.
We must live with hope, keep praying, worshipping day to day,
Keep believing God will bless us in his very special way.
And yes, patience is a virtue that helps us stay the course,
Through every living moment, life will prove God IS the source.
Obedience to let him take control and not do things our way,
That's one sure way for God to bring his blessings into play.
For that's how faith is tested and obedience will prove;
Keep holding on, do not give up, wait for God to make his move.
When you put your trust in God, and accept life through his grace,
You affirm that you believe in him and will one day see his face.
Remember Isaac and Abraham and the long walk to that hill—
And how God at the appointed hour, their need he did fulfill?
That is true faith and obedience—trust put to the test,
And when we wait upon the Lord, we will receive his best.
So, no matter how uncertain—or daunting you may feel,
Put your trust and faith in Jesus, believe that he is real.
And as we journey through our lifetime, living day by day,
God will prove his love and grace as he enlightens our way.

Luke 17:5 ESV

The apostles said to the Lord, "increase our faith."

Galatians 3:7 & 9 NLT

The real children of Abraham, then, are those who put their faith in God. What's more, the Scriptures looked forward to this time when God would make the Gentiles right in his sight because of their faith. God proclaimed this good news to Abraham long ago when he said, "All nations will be blessed through you."

Hebrews 11:1 & 6 KJV

Now faith is the substance of things hoped for, the evidence of things not seen. But without faith it is impossible to please him, for he that cometh to God must believe that he is a rewarder of them that seek him diligently.

Isaiah 55:8 NIV

For my thoughts are not your thoughts, neither are your ways my ways, declares the Lord.

"The greatest legacy you can pass on to your children and grandchildren is not your money or the other material things you have accumulated in life. The greatest legacy you can pass on to them is the legacy of your character and your faith."

—Reverend Billy Graham

Let Go and Trust God

We may not have all the answers for our purpose on this sphere,
But God surely did not put us here for anxiety and despair.
We learn to face what life brings, in this ever—changing world,
Praying humbly with peaceful joy and a very thankful soul.
Work hard at being happy and wisely let our worries go,
Keeping faith and trust alive through life's tumultuous flow.
Stay positive, rely and trust God always,
Thru good and bad give thanks with praise.
If we want our faith in God to blossom, we have to let it grow,
Trust in the Lord with all your heart and just let all our troubles go.

Matthew 6:25—27 NIV

Therefore, I tell you, do not worry about your life, what you will eat or drink;
or about your body, what you will wear. Is not life more than food,
and the body more than clothes?
Look at the birds of the air; they do not sow or reap or store away in barns,
and yet your heavenly Father feeds them.
Are you not much more valuable than they?
Can any one of you by worrying add a single hour to your life?

Proverbs 3:5 NIV

Trust in the Lord with all your heart and lean not on your
own understanding.

Psalm 25:20 KJV

O keep my soul and deliver me, let me not be ashamed, for I put my trust in thee.

Isaiah 26:3 KJV

Thou wilt keep him in perfect peace, whose mind is stayed on thee because he trusteth in thee.

"Some of us think holding on makes us strong,
but sometimes it is letting go."
—Herman Hesse

Exalt and Praise His Name

I came out of a wilderness and kneeled before God's throne,
My salvation came through Jesus, I could not do it on my own.
Just when I thought that I would die, felt like I could go on no more,
I cried out to my heavenly father and he opened wide the door.
Why did it cost half of my life to finally listen to his voice?
Most of the time I turned away, making the wrong choice.
I did not give my life to him or surrender heart and mind,
Just living out most of my days, spiritually deaf, dumb and blind.
Now today, before God's throne I bow, my voice to him I raise in praise,
I thank my Lord for Jesus and will exalt his name always.
To him be all the honor and glory for the rest of all my days.

Psalm 34:3 KJV

O magnify the Lord with me and let us exalt his name together.

Jeremiah 7:23 ESV

But this command I gave them; "Obey my voice, and I will be your God, and you shall be my people. And walk in all the way that I command you, that it may be well with you."

Hebrews 4:16 ESV

Let us then with confidence draw near to the throne of grace,
that we may receive mercy and find grace to help in time of need.

Exodus 15-2 KJV

The Lord is my strength and song and he is become my salvation. He is my God and I will prepare him an habitation, my father's God, and I will exalt him.

Psalm 92:1 NLT

It is a good thing to give thanks to the Lord and to sing praises to the Most High.

Isaiah 25:1 ESV

O Lord, you are my God; I will exalt you, I will praise your name, for you have done wonderful things, plans formed of old, faithful and sure.

"I will exalt you, my God the King,
I will praise your name for ever and ever.
 Every day I will praise you and extol your name for ever and ever. Great is the Lord and most worthy of praise, his greatness no one can fathom."

—KING DAVID # 145 NIV

Sow Seeds for a Joyful Harvest

When the joys of life are unfulfilled,
The hurt weighs heavy against your heart.
With pain so deep, despair, defeat,
It tears your heart and soul apart.
And now you feel broken, alone,
The pain too much for flesh and bone.
Yet, on what may seem barren fields today;
Hold faith steady, keep sowing in a holy way,
Just like a seed buried, covered in the earth,
The fruits of joy and peace will spring birth.
We have to plant these seeds in faith,
Trust in the Lord, be still and wait.
For God he knows our every need,
Trust in his words of life and let him lead.
Sow peace and joy and watch them grow,
For we will always reap the seeds we sow.

Galatians 6:7–8 KJV

Be not deceived, God is not mocked; for whatever a man soweth, that shall he reap.
For he that soweth to his flesh shall reap corruption, but he that soweth to the spirit shall of the spirit reap life everlasting.

2 Corinthians 9:6 KJV

But this I say, He which soweth sparingly shall reap also sparingly, and he which soweth bountifully shall reap also bountifully

Proverbs 11:24—25 NIV

One person gives freely, yet gains even more, another withholds unduly, but comes to poverty. A generous person will prosper; whoever refreshes others will be refreshed.

2 Corinthians 9:10 NIV

Now he who supplies seed to the sower and bread for food will supply and increase your store of seed and will enlarge the harvest of your righteousness.

"Don't judge each day by the harvest you reap but by the seeds that you plant."

—Robert Louis Stevenson

Seek God First—Trust Him

We all search ourselves for answers, through the challenges of life,
It seems like a constant struggle to quell the turmoil, calm the strife.
We must learn to listen to the Holy Spirit, to hear the call from deep inside,
And seek ye first the kingdom of Heaven and in God's will abide.
We should always trust in the Lord, never give up hope and faith,
Throughout the storms of life hold firm, as on the Lord we wait.
Lean on faith, live always—within the laws of God above,
Peace comes when we learn to live in his Awesome Grace—with Love.

Psalm 112:7 KJV

He shall not be afraid of evil tidings, his heart is fixed,
trusting in the Lord

Psalm 46:10 NIV

Be still, and know that I am God;
I will be exalted among the heathen,
I will be exalted in the earth.

Isaiah 12:2 ESV

Behold God is my salvation, I will trust and will not be afraid
for the Lord God is my strength and my song, and he has
become my salvation.

Psalm 40:4 KJV

Blessed is the man that maketh the Lord his trust and respecteth not the proud, nor such as turn aside to lies.

"Many believe; and I believe, that I have been designated for this work by God. In spite of my old age, I do not want to give it up. I work out of love for God and I put all my hope in Him."

—Michelangelo

Let God Decide

Decisions, changes throughout our lives bring anxiety, despair,
New terrain, unchartered paths, sometimes open doors to fear.
Never knowing what lies ahead, wait on God; trust him,
For that's how obedience to our Lord, truly will begin.
Keep trusting in God, believe he will always redeem,
No matter how daunting your past or future may seem.
Ask him to guide and lead you, show your true life's path,
Be sure to humbly listen and obey, when he speaks to your heart.
God knows what's ahead of us, only he knows the true way.
Through all trials, changes in our lives, we should trust him and obey.
Choose to live obediently, within God's laws abide,
Live in peace, be patient and always let our Lord decide.

James 1:5 ESV

If any of you lacks wisdom, let him ask God, who gives
generously to all without reproach, and it will be given him.

Psalm 18:28 KJV

For thou wilt light my candle, the Lord will enlighten my darkness.

Philippians 4:13 NLT

For I can do everything through Christ who gives me strength.

Psalm 31:3 KJV

For thou art my rock and fortress, therefore for thy names sake lead me and guide me.

But I came to learn that God never shows us something we aren't ready to understand. Instead, he lets us see what we need to see, when we are ready to see it. He'll wait until our eyes and hearts are open to him, and then when we're ready, he will plant our feet on the path that's best for us, but it's up to us to do the walking

—Immaculee Ilibagiza

Mirror Image

He Knows Our Every Need

Sometimes we feel hopeless, seems like life has hit a wall,
Our burdens feel so heavy, we are afraid that we might fall.
Some of us may actually think there is no one to turn to,
But hold off from that lying thought, for it certainly is not true.
Stop! Take a look in the mirror, no vanity—as humble as a child,
Stand there and imagine, just ponder for a while.
God made You, this image for his glory—HIS likeness, His All,
You are his divine creation, small, large, short or tall—
Believe you have his power, to break through any wall.
Your father sees; he knows your every need, before you even do.
And he will stand God Strong with you; when you believe it too.

Isaiah 43:7 KJV

Even every one that is called by my name,
for I have created him for my glory,
I have formed him, yea I have made him.

Matthew 18:3—4 ESV

Truly, I say to you, unless you turn and become like children, you will never enter the kingdom of heaven. Whoever humbles himself like this child is the greatest in the kingdom of heaven.

Matthew 11:29—30 NLT

Take my yoke upon you. Let me teach you, because I am humble and gentle at heart, and you will find rest for your souls.
For my yoke is easy to bear, and the burden I give you is light."

Matthew 6:8 ESV

Do not be like them, for your Father knows what you need before you ask him.

"Look in the mirror, go ahead and look yet again.
And look not at the reflection, for while this body of yours is marvelously complex in ways that continue to elude the reach of modern science, it is but a simple shell that holds the image of God within you. And if the shell is that grand, how much more what God has placed inside."

—CRAIG D. LOUNSBROUGH

Soar on His Wings

When our skies seem dark and hopeless,
And the world around us feels cold and grey,
We must stay focused on God's mercy,
Still giving thanks for this new day.
It's impossible to lift our tired wings,
When attempting takeoff on our own.
We must know that God is always with us,
Don't fly solo, no—we're not alone.
It may be overwhelming when dark clouds roll in,
Still we must persevere, to find God's strength within.
For if our hearts are filled with faith, trusting what God says,
The gloomy haze will give way, to better, brighter days.
Believe all God's promises, with hope, in trust sincere,
He will give you peace, joy and strength to overcome all fear.
Break free of your prison chains, knock down your old jail door—
With supernatural power, rise up and take off—fly high!
Reclaim your life and Soar!

Isaiah 42:7 KJV

To open the blind eyes, to bring out the prisoners from
prison and them that sit in darkness out of the prison house.

Isaiah 40:30—31 NIV

Even youths grow tired and weary and young men stumble and fall;
But those who hope in the Lord will renew their strength.
They will soar on wings like eagles. They will run and not grow weary.
They will walk and not faint.

Psalm 103:5 ESV

Who satisfies you with good so that your
youth is renewed like the eagles.

Psalm 142:7 KJV

Bring my soul out of prison, that I may praise thy name,
the righteous shall compass me about, for thou shalt
deal bountifully with me.

"When storms are coming, birds seek shelter.
The eagle alone avoids the storm by flying above it.
In the storms of life may you fly like an eagle and soar above."

—Anonymous

Stay Positive—Keep Moving On

On life's highway, when the journey gets long,
I always sing or hum my favorite song.
Whenever I begin to feel sad and blue,
I just try to do the things I love to do.
In doing this, I find joy and bliss,
I try to keep moving, no sad times to reminisce.
Thru the pathways I walk, the mountains I climb,
Conquering life's terrain, one step at a time.
I stay positive, hopeful, no longer feeling so blue,
With peace and joy, my heart and soul are renewed.

Proverbs 15:13 KJV

A merry heart maketh a cheerful countenance,
but by sorrow of the heart the spirit is broken.

Ephesians 4:23 ESV

And to be renewed in the spirit of your minds.

Psalm 51:12 KJV

Restore unto me the joy of thy salvation and uphold me
with thy free spirit.

"The journey of a thousand miles begins with one small step."
—Lao Tzu

Time Brings Brighter Days.

With time, the dark days will seem brighter,
Heavy burdens will feel a whole lot lighter.
It will take time for our wounds to heal,
Pray, ask God to soothe the pain we feel.
We cannot allow ourselves to perish,
Pondering only on pain and loss;
For sure, we will miss the flight,
Which puts us back on God's course.
Keep looking for the bright stars in the night,
Strive to change our inner darkness to light.
Never can we throw in the towel,
Nor ever should we give up the spiritual fight.
God gives clarity to enlighten each new day,
He will renew our souls along the narrow way.

Luke 1:79 ESV

To give light to those who sit in darkness and in the shadow of death, to guide our feet into the way of peace.

Isaiah 60:20 KJV

Thy sun shall no more go down, neither shall thy moon withdraw itself for the Lord shall be thine everlasting light and the days of thy mourning shall be ended.

Ecclesiastes 3:1 & 4 KJV

To everything there is a season and a time to every
purpose under the heaven. A time to weep and a
time to laugh, a time to mourn and a time to dance.

Lamentations 3:22—23 KJV

It is of the Lord's mercies that we are not consumed,
because of his compassions we fail not.
They are new every morning, great is thy faithfulness.

John 8:12 NLT

Jesus spoke to the people once more and said, "I am the light
of the world. If you follow me, you won't have to walk in darkness,
because you will have the light that leads to life."

"He that has light within his own clear breast may sit in the center, and
enjoy bright day—but he that hides a dark soul and foul thoughts,
benighted walks under the mid—day sun; himself his own dungeon."

—JOHN MILTON

A Prayer for Blessings and Guidance

Lord, I thank you for this life you've given to me,
I will try to be true and worthy of who you made me to be.
You know my heart's desires before I can even ask.
Yet still I ask, Lord—guidance, to fulfill my lifelong tasks.
Sometimes when I doubt and want to go it alone,
Or forget, and take my eyes off you on your throne;
Put me back on the course, help me take up the slack,
With you at the helm, I will be on the right track.
Lord, grant peace on my journey along life's way,
Guide me on the pathway to heavens highway.
I know I can ask for guidance, with faith to receive,
For you promised your blessings to those who believe.

Isaiah 58:11 NIV

The Lord will guide you always, he will satisfy your needs in
a sun—scorched land and will strengthen your frame.
You will be like a well—watered garden, like a spring whose waters
never fail.

Matthew 21:22 KJV

And all things, whatsoever ye shall ask in prayer believing,
ye shall receive.

John 16:13 ESV

When the Spirit of truth comes, he will guide you into all the truth, for he will not speak on his own authority, but whatever he hears he will speak, and he will declare to you the things that are to come.

Deuteronomy 28:8 KJV

The Lord shall command the blessing upon thee in thy storehouses and in all that thou settest thine hand unto and he shall bless thee in the land which the Lord thy God giveth thee.

Psalm 37:23 NLT

The Lord directs the steps of the godly. He delights in every detail of their lives.

"Be true to yourself, help others, make each day your masterpiece, make friendship a fine art, drink deeply from good books, especially the Bible, build a shelter against a rainy day, give thanks for your blessings and pray for guidance every day."

—John Wooden

Keep Me Today and Always—A Prayer

Oh, Master never let me go,
Lord, never let me fall.
Keep me close and walk with me,
My life is yours, in all.
Through night and day, I ask and pray,
With me you will forever stay.
In every action, thought and deed,
For life, I know you are all I need.
Show me life's pathway, straight and true,
To forever live my life with you.

Psalm 25:20 KJV

O keep my soul and deliver me, let me not
be ashamed, for I put my trust in thee.

Psalm 40:11 KJV

Withhold not thou thy tender mercies from me, O Lord,
let thy lovingkindness and thy truth continually preserve me.

Psalm 4:8 NLT

In peace I will lie down and sleep, for you alone, O Lord,
will keep me safe.

Psalm 16:1 NIV

Keep me safe, my God, for in you I take refuge.

"If God is your partner, make big plans."
—D.L Moody

Patience and Virtue—A Recipe for Life

Having Patience is a Virtue—it's a saying of old.
Deep in those words, great meaning unfolds.
When into a life these two are mixed in,
It gives birth to great Joy and Peace within.
For patience and virtue are surely divine,
A recipe for success when gently combined.
These two precious gifts you can't buy at the store,
Yet they are abundantly free when you abide in God's law.
Always live in God's light, be obedient and true,
And both these priceless life treasures,
Will come naturally—overflowing to you.

Hebrews 10:36 KJV

Ye have need of patience that after ye have done
the will of God, ye might receive the promise.

Psalm 37:7 NLT

Be still in the presence of the Lord and wait patiently
for him to act, don't worry about evil people who
prosper or fret about their wicked schemes.

2 Peter 1:5 KJV

And besides this, giving all diligence, add to your faith,
virtue and to your virtue, knowledge.

Philippians 4:8 KJV

Finally brethren, whatsoever things are true, whatsoever things are honest, whatsoever things are just, whatsoever things are lovely, whatsoever things are of a good report. If there be any virtue and if there be any praise, think on these things.

"Patience is a conquering virtue."
—Geoffrey Chaucer

Call on The Lord for Restoration

When your heart is troubled, and wolves howl at your door,
Remember, God is right beside you, just call on him some more.
The world we live in, would make us feel, we have no one to turn to,
But when you obey and trust the Lord, He comes—and lives with you.
Some people think this is insane; it's true! —God can restore it all,
Trust, believe, obey his word and he will never let you fall.
When it storms as though the road ahead is going to wash away,
Our heavenly father in his love will always find another way.
When you are down, to just a few crumbs on your plate,
The Lord will feed you, fill up your cup, when you overflow with faith.
Call on him for healing, when the prognosis says ailing health,
God knows that your well—being, is a great part of life's wealth.
And just when you are counting pennies or your pockets are almost bare,
He will increase you a thousand—fold, when in him you trust and fear.
That's how miracles truly happen, yet the world cannot perceive,
If only they would ask in faith, and totally believe—
The one who asks in faith and trust is the one who will receive.
Believe

Joel 2:25—26 ESV

I will restore to you the years that the swarming locust has eaten, the hopper, the destroyer, and the cutter, my great army, which I sent among you. You shall eat in plenty and be satisfied, and praise the name of the Lord your God, who has dealt wondrously with you. And my people shall never again be put to shame.

Matthew 7:7—8 KJV

Ask, and it shall be given you; seek, and ye shall find; knock, and it shall be opened unto you: For every one that asketh receiveth; and he that seeketh findeth; and to him that knocketh it shall be opened.

Acts 2:21 ESV

And it shall come to pass that everyone who calls upon the name of the Lord shall be saved.

Luke 1:50 KJV

And his mercy is on them that fear him from generation to generation.

Luke 1:37 ESV

For nothing will be impossible with God.

"All I have seen teaches me to trust the Creator for all I have not seen."
—RALPH WALDO EMERSON

God Bless Our Home

Lord, bless this place you gave us to call our home,
Little, log cabin—big city house—or a superdome.
Shelter and help us, forever shine light on our way.
Pray we rise happy and healthy, renewed every day.
Cover us safely when life's storms begin,
Lord, please protect every soul sheltered within.
Through our doors and windows shine your light always,
Feed, keep and bless us for the rest of our days.
Embrace us in your love and let your mercy be shown,
To the souls that abide here and all who enter our home.

Psalm 91:9–11 KJV

Because thou hast made the Lord which is my refuge even the highest thy habitation, there shall no evil befall thee, neither shall any plague come nigh thy dwelling.
For he shall give his angels charge over thee to keep thee in all thy ways.

Matthew 7:25 NLT

Though the rain comes in torrents and the floodwaters rise and the winds beat against that house, it won't collapse because it is built on bedrock.

Joshua 24:15 KJV

But as for me and my house, we will serve the Lord.

Psalm 127:1 ESV

Unless the Lord builds the house, those who build it labor in vain. Unless the Lord watches over the city, the watchman stays awake in vain.

2 Samuel 7:29 NIV

Now be pleased to bless the house of your servant, that it may continue forever in your sight; for you, Sovereign Lord, have spoken, and with your blessing the house of your servant will be blessed forever.

"Those blessings are sweetest that are won with prayer and worn with thanks."

—Thomas Goodwin

Hold on to the Lovelight—of The Cross

The Gospel Truth

The days ahead may seem hopeless,
Morning's brightness quickly fades to dim,
And today you may feel like just giving up,
Worn out, tired, the future appears so grim.
Hold on brother, sister, don't be so dark blue,
This is all deception, no! none of that is true.
Keep remembering you are God's child my Friend,
Look to the lovelight in his words, clearly, this is not the end.
God who made you loves you, he paid an awesome price for you,
When Jesus bled—dying on a cross, it was a Victory for Me and You!
Hold on to the love of Jesus on the cross, keep your hope and faith in Him,
No matter what—hold on to his truth, throughout life's thick and thin.
Life is not always pleasant; and when you feel sad or dark blue,
Open the lovelight of his words and read of his love for you.
Let his words of life flow through, to shine in your heart today,
God is the only truth, the only life—and the only righteous way.

John 1:4 NIV

In him was life, and that life was the light of all mankind.

John 8:12 NLT

Jesus spoke to the people once more and said, "I am the light of the world. If you follow me, you won't have to walk in darkness, because you will have the light that leads to life."

Psalm 27:1 KJV

The Lord is my light and salvation, whom shall I fear?
The Lord is the strength of my life, of whom shall I be afraid?

John 14:6 ESV

Jesus said to him, "I am the way, and the truth, and the life.
No one comes to the Father except through me.

John 3:17 NIV

For God did not send his Son into the world to condemn the world, but to save the world through him.

"Give light, and the darkness will disappear of itself."
—Desiderius Erasmus

A True—Life Miracle Story

I decided to share this true story—so you could read,
About two aging, beat up brothers of the same seed.
Sometimes having to struggle, stay afloat in life's brew,
We've had gladness, with sadness, then God gave us something new.
At times in the struggle we may forget to say "I love you,"
But deep down inside—though unsaid—love is true.
We live daily, taking much for granted, caught up in spin,
Not knowing how fragile—the veil between life and death is—so thin.
****
Brother, Last night when you told me you were going to die,
It was the first time in a long, long time I started to cry.
When you told me that the doctors said you were going away,
All I could remember was what Mom and Dad used to say,
That word came so easy, because they taught us to—Pray.
So now each day I pray more, I don't want to lose you,
When after half of a lifetime I am just getting to know you.
A Brother like you, life could never replace,
Warm, peaceful, gentle smiling face.
I know you are ready to go- you've been tired so long,
Having carried your burden, carried it strong.
I know through it all God has seen you along,
He is the one that is keeping you strong.
So come on little brother, don't give up the good fight,
God has blessed you with goodness, blessed you with light.
From our childhood to manhood we have seen all the signs,
We have seen good and evil, great miracles in time.
If God wants you right now, it would break my heart,
If you have to leave this earth, brothers having to part.
I know he has blessed us—he has given us so much,

He sustains us and keeps us just within his touch.
Yes, I remember what Mom and Dad used to say,
Truthfully, endlessly, let us continue to pray.
So, on my knees I will ask that he lets us hang tight,
For many more moons—time—to burn some daylight.
I will bow down and ask God for a miracle—in prayer,
And hope that in Heaven Mom and Dad echo it there.
Tonight, when I ask, I want you to ask too,
As I pray this pray especially for you.
But I need your help little brother, you pray better than me,
God used you, to show me, the power in a bended knee.
So, don't give up now Brother, pray—God willing, this too shall pass.
Let's kneel at Christ's cross and hold on to his staff.
I ask God to Grant us many more years in this life.
And thank him for the blessing of the miracle of life.

Isaiah 57:18 KJV

I have seen his ways and will heal him,
I will lead him also and restore comforts unto
him and to his mourners.

Jeremiah 17:14 ESV

Heal me, O Lord, and I shall be healed; save me,
and I shall be saved, for you are my praise.

James 5:15 NIV

And the prayer offered in faith will make the sick person well;
the Lord will raise them up. If they have sinned, they will be forgiven.

Note:
God heard and answered our prayers that night and in the years that followed.
Many years and many moons later, my brother passed away peacefully
at his home, shortly after his 56th birthday.
This was written days after the doctor gave him just a few months to live.
His miracle and powerful belief in a savior, brought me back to the cross.
He greatly inspired and encouraged me to complete this book.

Together we did "burn" and enjoy nine more years of God's blessed light. God gave us the miracle we prayed for.
The Miracle of Life.

For my Brother Leon.
11/19/1959–11/23/2014
—New York, NY

A New Life Portrait in Living Light—By God the Master Artist

I sat at my window that winter, just looking out at the world,
Some days felt so depressing, dark, dreary and cold.
Time and joy always froze, staring at this lifeless picture,
Vista so grim—outside my window loomed an uncertain future.
It was a time when I felt lost and tired; I could not find my way,
And I would walk and talk to the Lord on those dark, solemn days.
Then one day it all changed suddenly, I beheld life with new sight,
The old scenery awoke, the dark skies lit up with sunlight.
The sleeping trees started to awake with life's renewed surge,
The white, frozen Tundra receded, as the green earth emerged.
The scene came alive as squawking ducks streaked across.
I watched, every morning, this ever changing, living portrait —
I pondered the source.
Who can change ashes for joy, death to life, darkness to light?
Only a Master Artist can create a new day with such awesome might.
I knew there and then, he would help me find my way,
He is the creator, renewing, restoring, creating night and day
I learned we must trust God, when we pray for light in our world,
I had to submit and surrender to him; bare the canvas of my soul.
When you humbly give God your heart, believe; and call on his name,
You will never have to walk alone or live in darkness again.

1 John 1:5 NIV

This is the message we have heard from him and declare to you;
God is light; in him there is no darkness at all.

A New Life Portrait in Living Light—By God the Master Artist

Isaiah 43:19 KJV

Behold, I will do a new thing, now it shall spring forth, shall ye not know it? I will even make a way in the wilderness, and rivers in the desert.

Psalm 18:28 ESV

For it is you who light my lamp; the Lord my God lightens my darkness.

2 Corinthians 4:6 NIV

For God, who said, "Let light shine out of darkness," made his light shine in our hearts to give us the light of the knowledge of God's glory displayed in the face of Christ.

Psalm 19:1 KJV

The heavens declare the glory of God and the firmament sheweth his handiwork.

"God is the Master Artist painting the picture of your life, and he sees the whole canvas."

—Elisa Pulliam

A Friend + A Buddy = A Fuddy

I thank God for blessing me with my Buddy, my Friend,
A friend who like no other, has stuck with me to the end.
Like brothers during childhood, together through bad and good,
Throughout all life's challenges, our friendship has withstood.
Oh Lord I know that I am blessed to have this faithful friend,
For this eternal bond of love, only you can send.
And while some friends have left us, some have flown away,
Our bond keeps growing stronger still, even though we are miles away.
I praise you Lord for friendship—for me and my Fuddy I pray—
You let us share this God Blessed love, Forever and Always.

Proverbs 18:24 KJV

A man that hath friends must shew himself friendly
and there is a friend that sticketh closer than a brother.

Proverbs 27:9 ESV

Oil and perfume make the heart glad, and the sweetness of a friend
comes from his earnest counsel.

Romans 12:10 NLT

Love each other with genuine affection, and take delight
in honoring each other.

Psalm 133: 1 KJV

Behold, how good and how pleasant it is for brethren to dwell together in unity.

"Friendship is the only cement that will ever hold the world together."
—Woodrow Wilson

For Winston, Gemma, Kerri and Adrian
—TNT West Indies

Mercy and Compassion—Praise Him

Joyfully give God praise,
Hearts, voices thankfully raise.
Show him all honor, give glory,
Say thanks for your life's story.
Keep trusting with faith,
Patience as we wait.
Exalt him, invite him in.
Accept him, to abide within.
Glorify him in love, great exultation,
Give praise for mercy, saving compassion.
Praise Him!

Psalm 7:17 KJV

I will praise the Lord according to his righteousness
and will sing praise to the name of the Lord most high.

1 Timothy 1:17 NIV

Now to the King eternal, immortal, invisible, the only God,
be honor and glory for ever and ever. Amen.

Psalm 48:1 ESV

Great is the Lord and greatly to be praised in the
city of our God.

Psalm 145:3 NLT

Great is the Lord! He is most worthy of praise!
No one can measure his greatness.

"I will have mercy on whom I will have mercy,
and I will have compassion on whom I will have compassion."

—GOD
   Exodus 33:19

Together Always—Never Alone

In Darkness and in Light

Out of night's darkness always comes a new morn,
Warming light gives shape to horizons, with each new dawn.
Celestial sun to warm and illuminate the way,
God's awesome power, heralding each brand, new day.
And as we awake and stand upon the earth,
Give God the thanks for renewed life—rebirth.
For we are graced; highly favored, day and night,
Blessed to awake, to live in God's awesome might.
So, rise up, with thanks, welcome God's divine embrace,
Reach for the warmth of his love, his lifesaving grace.
Remember, whenever you are sad or burdened with sorrow,
Hope comes like renewed light for today and tomorrow.
For each brand—new day with its warming light,
Is a shining beacon of God's power, his eternal might.
He is in the darkness and He is the light,
All around us, within us, to our left, to our right.
So reach out to him now, you are not on your own.
He is with you always, and you will never walk alone.

Psalm 36:9 NIV

For with you is the fountain of life; in your light we see light.

Isaiah 43:2 KJV

When thou passest through the waters,
I will be with thee and through the rivers,
they shall not overflow thee,
when thou walkest through the fire, thou shalt not be
burned, neither shall the flame kindle upon thee.

Deuteronomy 31:6 ESV

Be strong and courageous. Do not fear or be in dread of them,
for it is the Lord your God who goes with you.
He will not leave you or forsake you."

"I will love the light for it shows me the way, yet I will
endure the darkness because it shows me the stars."

—Augustine "Og" Mandino

Sunbeam Smile—Happy Birthday

Your blue eyes sometimes give us a glimpse of your soul.
A life's story if read from deep within—bittersweet unfolds.
You bless us rarely with your Sunbeam Smile— it is so divine,
I cross my heart, your smile is like warm, bright sunshine.
I really think that sweet smile, can open heaven's door,
I wish you'd smile more often and bless us some more.
We know your smile and laughter comes from your heart.
Whatever you've faced in life, God's been with you from the start.
He must love you, to bless you with the length of days,
For he has securely, safely kept you, in his goodness always.
We ask blessings as we sit down for this, your Birthday Feast,
Pray you keep drinking from the fountain of joy and peace,
Embrace happiness and laughter, may your spirit always soar.
And on this your special day, I pray to God—
He grants all you pray for, ever wish for—and more.

Psalm 20:4 NIV

May He give you the desire of your heart and
make all your plans succeed.

Proverbs 9:11 ESV

For by me your days will be multiplied,
and years will be added to your life.

Sunbeam Smile—Happy Birthday

Numbers 6:24—26 KJV

The Lord bless thee, and keep thee; the Lord make his face shine
upon thee, and be gracious unto thee;
The Lord lift up his countenance
upon thee, and give thee peace.

"God gave us the gift of life—it is up to us to
give ourselves the gift of living well,"

—Voltaire

For my Friend Bonnie.
09/08/1937–10/23/2018
—Stokesdale NC—USA

Take My Hand

My Lord, my Shepherd, today I ask,
Please take hold of my hand.
Walk with me and talk with me,
Lord guide me through this land.
O Lord I pray this very day,
With me through night and day you'll stay.
Grant me peace and let me see,
Your blessed mercies eternally.
I will live in hope for the day I see your face,
Until then, guide me, through this fleeting place.
Through life's hills and vales, Lord hold my hand,
Lead me home, into the Eternal land.

Isaiah 41:13 KJV

For I the Lord thy God will hold thy right hand,
saying unto thee, fear not, I will help thee.

Isaiah 52:12 NIV

But you will not leave in haste or go in flight; for the Lord will
go before you, the God of Israel will be your rear guard.

Psalm 48:14 KJV

For this is our God forever and ever,
he will be our guide even unto death.

Job 12:10 NIV

In his hand is the life of every creature
and the breath of all mankind.

"I have held many things in my hands,
and I have lost them all—but whatever I have
placed in God's hands, that I still possess."

—Martin Luther

Farewell My Brother

Goodbye, little Brother, I won't see you anymore,
For the rest of my life, I'll never hear you knock on my door.
I can't pick up the phone now, and just call you up,
We will never sit on the deck and drink from the cup.
We said our final goodbye, last moment, together in time,
Never knowing our last handshake was God Blessed—sublime.
My Brother; your memory will always live in my heart,
Till we travel in time to meet in a new world, new start.
If only I knew you were going away that day,
I would have hugged you, kissed you and begged God, you stay.
In life's trials and journeys, we are blessed here on earth,
A great blessing my brother, was having known you from birth.
Today we pause for a moment to remember you,
To sojourn for a time as we say farewell, adieu.
If you were here, I know exactly what you'd say,
Yes—we will keep on living— "tomorrow's a new day."
You won't want us bleeding and hurting inside,
Bogged down in sorrow, not riding life's high tide.
As time keeps on flowing, the hurt, God will heal,
The memories of brotherhood—time passages seal.
I hope to see you in the crowd, hear you in the wind.
Time will soothe our souls, heal the grief, pain within.
Go fly with the angels brother, fly far from your pain.
We will always love you—forever and again.

1 Thessalonians 4:13-14 NIV

Brothers and sisters, we do not want you to be uninformed about those who sleep in death, so that you do not grieve like the rest of mankind, who have no hope. For we believe that Jesus died and rose again, and so we believe that God will bring with Jesus those who have fallen asleep in him.

Matthew 5:4 KJV

Blessed are they that mourn, for they shall be comforted.

Isaiah 57:1 NIV

The righteous perish, and no one takes it to heart; the devout are taken away, and no one understands that the righteous are taken away to be spared from evil.

John 16:22 NLT

"So you have sorrow now, but I will see you again; then you will rejoice, and no one can rob you of that joy."
Jesus

"The pain of parting is nothing to the joy of meeting again."

—CHARLES DICKENS

For my Brother Wayne 5/27/1961–3/26/2001
—HOLLYWOOD FL- USA

Keep the Faith—Ride Life's Tide

At times it feels impossible to hold on to our faith,
It's as though all we ever do is pray and trust and wait.
But this is exactly how patience is taught,
While the spiritual battles in life are fought,
This is the way everlasting faith is perfected,
The foundation on which pure dependence is wrought.
If we were to build our lives on shifting sand and doubt,
When the mighty tides of life roar in,
they would surely knock us out.
And if our faith has any indecisive cracks,
Life's storms will always, knock us on our backs.
So, keep believing, trusting God with faith,
Hold fast, keep riding on in hope, for God is never late.
Persevere and endure, do not fall away to the side,
Grasp tightly to Faith and ride out life's tide.

Revelation 2:25—26 NLT

I will ask nothing more of you except that you hold tightly to what you have until I come. To all who are victorious, who obey me to the very end, to them I will give authority over all the nations.

Joshua 23:8 NIV

But you are to hold fast to the Lord your God, as you have until now.

Romans 4:20—21 NLT

Abraham never wavered in believing God's promise. In fact,
his faith grew stronger, and in this he brought glory to God.
He was fully convinced that God is able to do whatever he promises.

Matthew 11:6 NLT

And he added;
"God blesses those who do not fall away because of me."

"The only limit to our realization of tomorrow will be our doubts of today. Let us move forward with strong and active faith."

—Franklin D. Roosevelt

True Love Lives On

I put my trust in someone I valued more than just a friend,
That's when I opened up my heart and got it slammed again.
Just when I thought I built a wall and grew a brand, new shell,
I let the world come in, betray my trust, it hurt my heart like hell.
But while I sat there bleeding, a lesson came to mind,
I learned, we cannot stop living, loving—trusting in mankind.
We must move on with the wisdom, earned from each past step,
Living life with full passion, forgiveness, no regret.
So now I know I must get up—to go forward on the course,
I have to shake off betrayal, lose sadness, toss the loss.
I am learning how to open up and keep a tender heart,
And walk along the worldly road without getting ripped apart.
I will not let hurt stop me, or coldness turn my heart to stone,
I'll surely not give up on love, in the days I walk alone.
I will keep my heart warm with God's love and hold fast to my faith,
For the True Love God has in store for me is surely worth the wait.

1 John 4:7 NIV

Dear friends, let us love one another, for love comes from God.
Everyone who loves has been born of God and knows God.

Ephesians 5:2 ESV

And walk in love, as Christ loved us and gave himself up for us,
a fragrant offering and sacrifice to God.

Proverbs 31:10—12 & 30 KJV

Who can find a virtuous woman? for her price is far above rubies.
The heart of her husband doth safely trust her, so that he shall
have no need of spoil.
She will do him good and not evil all the days of her life
Favor is deceitful and beauty is vain, but a woman that feareth the Lord, she shall be praised.

Psalm 1:1—3 KJV

Blessed is the man that walketh not in the counsel of the ungodly nor standeth in the way of sinners, nor sitteth in the seat of the scornful. And he shall be like a tree planted by the rivers of water that bringeth forth his fruit in his season, his leaf also shall not wither and whatsoever he doeth shall prosper.

"There is no remedy for love but to love more."

—Henry David Thoreau

Thank You for More Than Enough—Everyday

We thank you Lord for each new day,
For a warm dry place, a bed to lay.
For a meal to eat and clothes to wear,
To have been blessed with yet another year.
Thank you, Lord, for our good health,
These gifts to us are priceless wealth.
But most of all we thank you Lord,
Forever always—being near.
We thank you for each brand—new day,
Blessed with your peace, love and good cheer.

Psalm 106:1 KJV

Praise ye the Lord, O give thanks unto the Lord for he is good and his mercy endureth forever.

Psalm 26:7 NLT

Singing a song of thanksgiving and telling of all your wonders.

Philippians 4:6—7 ESV

Do not be anxious about anything, but in everything by prayer and supplication with thanksgiving let your requests be made known to God. And the peace of God, which surpasses all understanding, will guard your hearts and your minds in Christ Jesus.

Thank You for More Than Enough—Everyday

"I can no other answer make but thanks, and thanks, and ever thanks."
—William Shakespeare

Choose Eternity Wisely

We stand here at life's crossroads, where a choice has to be made.
Do we abide in the heavenly spirit, allow earth's vanities to fade?
Or do we embrace the luring calls of this our temporal world?
The choice you make friend, is worth your life, your very sacred soul.
The strong allure of worldly pleasures forever will exist,
The desire for self—gratification, we must steadfastly resist.
God's law has long been handed down, and in stone was firmly set,
Truly, the wages of sin are paid for— with eternal, spiritual death.
The only choice that we can make to embrace life's purest joy and beauty,
Is to stay within God's guiding light—we should choose His eternity.
Never can we lose our lives for a pound of flesh, so mere,
When our souls can live forever, if our Lord we love and fear.
To live a life so full of God's promises, in peace and joy—forever dwell.
What would you my Brother, Sister—choose today?
Heaven's Eternity or Hell's?

Matthew 16:25—26 KJV

For whosoever shall save his life shall lose it and whosoever shall lose his life for my sake shall find it.
For what is a man profited if he shall gain the whole world and lose his own soul?
Or what shall a man give in exchange for his soul?

Choose Eternity Wisely

Deuteronomy 30:19 NIV

This day I call the heavens and the earth as witnesses against you that I have set before you life and death, blessings and curses. Now choose life, so that you and your children may live

1 John 2:17 ESV

And the world is passing away along with its desires, but whoever does the will of God abides forever.

James 1:14—16 KJV

But every man is tempted, when he is drawn
away of his own lust and enticed.
Then when lust hath conceived, it bringeth
forth sin and sin, when it is finished, bringeth forth death.
Do not err, my beloved children.

"The strongest principle of our growth lies in human choice."

—George Eliot

Ingredients for a Happy Life—A Prayer

O Lord, I ask for *Wisdom*, when I have to make a choice.
Bless me with your *Guidance*, grant me *Peace* to hear your voice.
O Father give me *Knowledge, Courage, Strength* to fulfill your plan.
Grant me a heart, full of *Love*, with *Time* to spread throughout this land.
Sprinkle me with *Patience*, bless me with *Good Health*,
And if your *Grace* allows for me, mix in a dash of *Wealth*.
Serenity and *Comfort*, *Faithful Friends* I ask of you.
Peace, Joy, Happiness and love that's always true.
Lead me through *Obedience* to always do your will,
For sure with these life ingredients, my life will be fulfilled.

Galatians 5:22—23 NLT

But the Holy Spirit produces this kind of fruit in our lives, love, joy, peace, patience, kindness, goodness, faithfulness, gentleness, and self—control.

2 Corinthians 8:7 ESV

But as you excel in everything; in faith, in speech, in knowledge, in all earnestness, and in our love for you; see that you excel in this act of grace also.

2 Chronicles 1:12 KJV

Wisdom and Knowledge is granted unto thee and I will give
thee riches and wealth and honor as none of the kings have
had before, neither shall they have after thee.

John 4:14 NLT

But those who drink the water I give will never be thirsty again.
It becomes a fresh, bubbling spring within them, giving them eternal life.

Jeremiah 33:6 KJV

Behold I will bring it health and cure and I will cure them and will
reveal unto them the abundance of peace and truth.

"God is not accustomed to refusing a good gift to those who ask.
Since he is good, and especially to those who are faithful to him,
we should hold fast to him with all our soul, our heart, our strength,
and so, enjoy his light and see his glory and possess the grace
of his supernatural joy."

—SAINT AMBROSE

Angels of The Heavenly King—On Earth

I barely awoke that morning, hardly alive to face another day,
I questioned my fallen spirit—why does my soul still stay?
Laying in a hospital bed, in the middle of that night,
I hovered within death's dark, cold grip, I could not see the light.
Preparing to say goodbye to life, about to lose my destiny,
Why! I was just beginning to enjoy life's vast humanity.
As the days wore on, I barely struggled, almost giving up the fight,
Only my mortality stared back, like a dark, dead cold night.
Just when it was coldest and darkest, survival so slim,
My faith and hope quickly receding, my breath drawing thin—
God sent me an Angel—YOU—Sent in HIS grace,
To restore my faith, second chance to rejoin the human race.
The kindness of your spirit brought healing—an Angelic Embrace,
Your compassion breathed the warmth of life, back into my face.
Because of your goodness I awoke to a bright new day,
Your love unraveled the mystery of my soul having stayed.
Through your mercy, you plucked me from fast sinking sand,
A message from God—His Love—sent in your caring hand.
Through you, he opened life's doors, when I thought they were sealed,
Yes, God blessed you with great power to help mankind heal.
So, today I go on living my life with spiritual sight.
My vision has changed, I see life clearly, through God's love light.
You my Angel, have proved, that love conquers the ills of this life,
God's love in, and through you, restoring my own life.
I will live always knowing, as long as life keeps on flowing,
That right here on this earth, if you take the time to look around,
You will surely discover that God's Angels abound.

Matthew 25:35—40 ESV

For I was hungry and you gave me food, I was thirsty and you gave me drink, I was a stranger and you welcomed me, I was naked and you clothed me, I was sick and you visited me, I was in prison and you came to me.
Then the righteous will answer him, saying, Lord, when did we see you hungry and feed you, or thirsty and give you drink? And when did we see you a stranger and welcome you, or naked and clothe you? And when did we see you sick or in prison and visit you? And the King will answer them,
Truly, I say to you, as you did it to one of the least of these my brothers, you did it to me.

Hebrews 13:2 NLT

Don't forget to show hospitality to strangers, for some who have done this have entertained angels without realizing it!

"Blessed are the merciful, for they will be shown mercy."

—Jesus Christ of Nazareth

You Get to Choose Your State of Mind

If you are feeling down,
Your face may wear a frown.
Just keep in mind you have a choice,
Of what you wear and how you sound.
You can choose hope and wear a smile,
Be of good cheer, happy all the while,
Or wear a frown or cry a tear,
And live all your life in sad despair.
Your choice.

Proverbs 15:13 NIV

A happy heart makes the face cheerful, but heartache crushes the spirit.

Romans 12:12 NIV

Be joyful in hope, patient in affliction, faithful in prayer.

Proverbs 15:30 NLT

A cheerful look brings joy to the heart,
good news makes for good health

Proverbs 17:22 KJV

A merry heart doeth good like a medicine,
but a broken spirit drieth the bones.

"Most folks are as happy as they make their minds up to be."
—Abraham Lincoln

The Blessings of True Love Await

My heart is afraid to love again,
Numbed by the pain of human hurt,
Too frozen to feel the sweet joy of true love,
Don't want my heart dragged through the dirt.
No contest between loneliness so dark,
And love's companionship, so bright,
So why do I still keep from choosing to love,
And slip away from its heartwarming light?
God knows I've been on a long, rough, one—sided road,
My trust broken, heart, too worn out to try,
Yet, loneliness keeps catching up as life keeps passing by.
I know when God created man,
He also created woman, to be his wife,
So neither of them would ever be alone,
And would have companionship throughout life.
Today I trust in God to heal my wounded heart,
Under his control, I know my love will not be torn apart.
I will trust in God, his path to true love I will follow,
Whatever his will for me—today or tomorrow.

Genesis 2:18 ESV

Then the Lord God said, "It is not good that the man should be alone; I will make him a helper fit for him.

The Blessings of True Love Await

Ecclesiastes 9:9 NLT

Live happily with the woman you love through all the meaningless days of life that God has given you under the sun,
The wife God gives you is your reward for all your earthly toil.

Proverbs 19:14 KJV

Houses and riches are the inheritance of fathers and a prudent wife is from the Lord.

Mark 10:6—9 ESV

But from the beginning of creation, God made them male and female. Therefore, a man shall leave his father and mother and hold fast to his wife, and the two shall become one flesh. So, they are no longer two but one flesh. What therefore God has joined together, let not man separate.

"I was made and meant to look for you and wait for you
and to become yours forever."

—Robert Browning

Loving Like God Loves—One Blood

Real Love is so awesome, just too vast to describe,
Sung, acted out through the ages, dissected by wise scribes.
We all seek the perfect formula for loving all mankind,
Searching without God's word, the spirit of love, we will never find.
The simple answer lies right before us and still we cannot see,
No! not until we don a Servants' Heart and live with Humility.
The key to love lies in the Word, handed down from God above.
The answer—we must follow Christ, and mirror God's pure love.
Through God's eyes of love, we would be Brothers and Sisters on Earth,
Respecting one another—seeing the Equality, in the Miracle of Birth.
God's love is not puffed up, selfish, nor is it vain,
His love has a way to grant Forgiveness, removing all life's stains.
True love vies for Peace, a Universal Brotherhood,
Up—rooting the world's evil and replanting life with good.
True love is experienced in the joy and laughter—the tears,
It thrives and grows stronger when these emotions we all share.
Through the eyes of God's love there would be no more war,
Discord would be replaced by Joy, Peace and Love shore to shore.
God's true love does not distinguish between rich and poor,
We will all enter Paradise or Hades through the same appointed door.
God's love sees no color, red, yellow, black, white,
God's himself created us ALL—we are HIS children, in his sight.
The flocks of God's heavenly church would never segregate,
For the love of God can never flourish in conflict or with hate.
If mankind must grow and blossom, to live in Universal Love,
We must Embrace the world with the love poured out by Christ above.
For God in sacrificial love, through his one son, paid the ultimate price,
When Pure Love flowed out in the BLOOD of our Lord—Our Savior Jesus Christ.

That is the Greatest Love of all, awesome, humbling, passionate, true,
God sacrificed his only son, pouring out his blood in love for Me and You.
Forever God's love lives on in our blood, its power must keep growing,
For through the veins of all Mankind, Christ's DNA keeps flowing.
So, no more envy, no more vanity, no hate, no more war,
See no inequality, never judging, just caring, loving— rich and poor.
Live to love like God loves all his children—
The Human Race of Earth.
All inoculated with the blood of Jesus Christ–
Through the Miracle of Birth.
* Love on Brethren*

Revelation 5:9 NIV

And they sang a new song, saying; "You are worthy to take the scroll and to open its seals, because you were slain, and with your blood you purchased for God persons from every tribe and language and people and nation.

Acts 20:28 KJV

Take heed therefore unto yourselves, and to all the flock, over which the Holy Ghost hath made you overseers, to feed the church of God, which he hath purchased with his blood.

Matthew 22:38—40 KJV

This is the first and great commandment.
And the second is like unto it, thou shalt love thy neighbor as thyself.
on these two commandments hang all the law and the prophets.

Psalm 133:1 NIV

How good and pleasant it is when God's people live together in unity!

"The Universal Brotherhood of man is our most precious possession, what there is of it."

—Mark Twain

Peace Be unto You—A Prayer of Thanks.

Heavenly Father, I come to you today,
To you my Lord I bow, to you my God I pray.
Thank you for my life, gracefully blessed.
Thanks to you Jesus, you give me sweet rest.
I thank you for the blessings of food and shelter,
Peace, so far away from a world of helter—skelter.
I praise you for the love you send,
I thank you for the friends Godsent.
Glory to you for my chariot to ride,
In your grace and forgiveness let me always abide.
Thank you for angels through the darkest night,
For a new morn, that brings the warming light.
I thank you for restoring my soul, healing my body,
For hanging out with me when I am feeling lonely.
I will pray and give thanks always, for this abundant share,
Of peace, joy and mercy, all my life in your care.

Luke 24:36 KJV

And as they thus spoke, Jesus himself stood
in the midst of them and saith unto them,
Peace be unto you.

Exodus 23:25 ESV

You shall serve the Lord your God, and he will bless your bread
and your water, and I will take sickness away from among you.

Leviticus 26:3–6 NLT

If you follow my decrees and are careful to obey my commands,
I will send you the seasonal rains. The land will then yield its crops,
and the trees of the field will produce their fruit. Your threshing season
will overlap with the grape harvest, and your grape harvest will overlap with
the season of planting grain. You will eat your fill and live securely in your
own land. I will give you peace in the land, and you will be able to sleep with
no cause for fear. I will rid the land of wild animals and keep your enemies out
of your land.

Psalm 72:7 KJV

In his days shall the righteous flourish and the abundance of peace,
so long as the moon endureth.

"A regenerated person should have an unspeakable peace in his spirit."
—Watchman Nee.

The Blood of Forgiveness—A Prayer

Father I ask forgiveness, keep me from sin I pray.
Forgive me for the times I err, for when I stray away.
Thanks for cleansing and forgiving me—every time I sin,
For your sword to fight temptation, to overcome, to win.
Thanks for the conviction in my heart, that tells me when I go wrong.
Thank you for a chance to change my ways, to grow up, to stand strong.
Help me resist the knock of sin, just outside my door.
Guide me heavenly father to always stay within your laws.
As I grow spiritually Lord, grant wisdom to make the proper choice,
Lead me to obedience, to seek and hear your guiding voice.
I will forever thank you Father, your blood has set me free,
I thank you for forgiveness, and your endless love for me.

1 John 1:9 KJV

If we confess our sins, he is faithful and just to forgive us
our sins and to cleanse us from all unrighteousness.

Proverbs 28:13 NIV

Whoever conceals their sins does not prosper, but the one who
confesses and renounces them finds mercy.

Ephesians 1:7 KJV

In whom we have redemption through his blood,
the forgiveness of sins, according to the riches of his grace.

Psalm 86:5 KJV

For thou Lord art good and ready to forgive and plenteous in mercy unto them that call upon thee.

"If God was not willing to forgive sin, heaven would be empty."
—German Proverb

Jesus is Always There

Whenever I feel sad and blue,
Lord, I try my best to think of you.
For when I focus on your ways,
My gloomy feelings lift away.
And when I think I am all alone,
Feeling a little down and cold,
I remind myself that you are here,
You live in me, within my soul.
I exist through you, not on my own,
And I will never, ever walk alone.

1 Corinthians 3:16 NLT

Don't you realize that all of you together are the temple of God and that the Spirit of God lives in you?

Hebrews 13:5 KJV

Let your conversation be without covetousness; and be content with such things as ye have; for he hath said, I will never leave thee, nor forsake thee.

John 14:20 ESV

In that day you will know that I am in my Father, and you in me, and I in you.

"And teaching them to obey everything I have commanded you. And surely, I am with you always, to the very end of the age."

—Jesus Christ

You are My Everything—A Prayer

Lord, you are my everything,
I want to thank you; praises sing.
You opened my eyes so I could see,
I feel your saving works alive in me.
When I feel lost or I sense my fear,
I remind myself you are always near.
Thanks for the fellowship we share,
For showing me my purpose here.
You take care of my everything,
I live within the peace this brings.
I am blessed by your love for me,
My guiding light you will forever be.
Teach me to hear and obey your call,
You are my strength, my life, my all.

Psalm 48:14 NLT

For that is what God is like. He is our God forever and ever, and he will guide us until we die.

Psalm 46:1—2 ESV

God is our refuge and strength, a very present help in trouble. Therefore, we will not fear though the earth gives way, though the mountains be moved into the heart of the sea,

Psalm 16:1—2 NIV

Keep me safe, my God, for in you I take refuge. I say to the Lord, "You are my Lord; apart from you I have no good thing."

"But the Lord watches over us every moment of every day.
He is there and He cares about every step and every breath."

—Dillon Burroughs.

A New Praise Song—Love Song Prayer

Oh Lord, I pray for mercy throughout the coming years,
For Strength, Hope and Courage to overcome my crippling fears.
Father, renew my waning joy, restore my forlorn soul,
You are the only hope I have in this whole, wide world.
O Holy God, my Father, do not let me fail you now,
To you alone I kneel, to you alone I bow.
Lord heal my soul, and calm my fears,
Forgive me and bless me, dry my tears.
Fill my life with joy, peace and laughter,
Walk with me always, hand in hand to my future.
From today on with love, a new song I will sing,
I will praise and love you, no matter what life may bring.

Psalm 40:2-3 NIV

He lifted me out of the slimy pit, out of the mud and mire,
he set my feet on a rock and gave me a firm place to stand.
He put a new song in my mouth, a hymn of praise to our God,
Many will see and fear and shall put their trust in him.

Isaiah 42:10 KJV

Sing unto the Lord a new song,
and his praise from the end of the earth,
ye that go down to the sea and all that is therein,
the isles and the inhabitants thereof.

Psalm 96:1—2 ESV

O sing to the Lord a new song; sing to the Lord, all the earth!
Sing to the Lord, bless his name, tell of his salvation from day to day.

Psalm 7:24—25 KJV

Thou shalt guide me with thy counsel and afterward
receive me to glory.
Whom have I in heaven but thee?
And there is none upon earth that I desire beside thee.

"Praise is the rehearsal of our eternal song,
by grace we learn to sing, and in glory we continue to sing."

—Charles Spurgeon

Spiritual Sight—The Love Walk

Imagine living every day, seeing God's love in plain sight,
Growing spiritually in peace and joy, every day and night.
This blessing only comes with a desire pure and true,
A yearning for God's presence; for his love to shine in you.
This calming love walk, it comes through constant prayer,
Learning to talk to God each hour, every day, year into year.
Keep straight on Eternal Street and you will not lose your way,
Don't get stuck in trendy traffic jams on Main Street today.
Keep focused on God's love, forever put him first,
For his wisdom and fellowship, always be athirst.
Stay close to the savior as you both walk and talk.
You, growing stronger in spirit, as you share his love walk.

Ezekiel 36:27 KJV

And I will put my spirit within you and cause you to walk in my statutes and ye shall keep my judgements and do them.

Psalm 51:10 NLT

Create in me a clean heart, O God. Renew a loyal spirit within me.

2 Kings 6:17 KJV

And Elisha prayed, and said, Lord, I pray thee, open his eyes that he may see. And the Lord opened the eyes of the young man, and he saw and behold, the mountain was full of horses and chariots of fire round about Elisha.

Ephesians 1:18 NIV

I pray that the eyes of your heart may be enlightened in order that you may know the hope to which he has called you, the riches of his glorious inheritance in his holy people,

"The eye through which I see God is the same eye through which God sees me, my eye and God's eye are one eye, one seeing, one knowing, one love."

—Meister Eckhart

Universal Soldiers—In the Service of The King

When I came to you and knocked, you opened your door.
Although you never knew me, or saw my face before.
And through God's love and mercy deep in your heart,
You let me in and blessed my life with a brand, new start.
You friend—are a Universal Soldier in the service of the king.
Remember the great ancient hymn or parents used to sing?

[It should be —A Universal Christian, Soldier's Creed]

> "In Christ there is no East or West.
> In him no South or North,
> But one great fellowship of Love,
> Throughout the whole round earth."
>
> John Oxenham- 1852–1941

So, let us embrace mankind in fellowship—Victory Evermore!
Through mercy, love and hope divine—to open doors on every shore.
Keep fighting Christian soldier, keep marching as to war,
Keep lifting souls for Jesus, praise and serve him evermore.
Serving mankind's fallen, God's soldiers march through hill and vale,
Redirecting lost, wounded, precious souls back on heavens narrow trail.
This is the God given mission, for the soldiers of our Lord,
To bring hope and light through fellowship, to lift more souls aboard.
Yeah, love my Sister, help my Brother, strengthen, encourage one another.
And though we fight in places far; trenches, oceans, different zones,
Universal soldiers in God's Army know they never fight alone.

Gird up with faith and courage, press on to eternity,
Hold true to heart and pure in soul, live forever through God's victory.
Our King is invincible.
All Hail the King!

Revelation 21:7 NIV

Those who are victorious will inherit all this, and I will
be their God and they will be my children.

Galatians 6:1—2 KJV

Brethren if a man be overtaken in a fault, ye which are spiritual,
restore such an one in the spirit of meekness, considering thyself
lest thou also be tempted.
Bear ye one another's burdens and so fulfill the law of Christ.

Psalm 116:5—6 ESV

Gracious is the Lord, and righteous; our God is merciful.
The Lord preserves the simple; when I was brought low, he saved me.

2 Corinthians 10:3—4 NIV

For though we live in the world, we do not wage war as the world does.
The weapons we fight with are not the weapons of the world. On the
contrary, they have divine power to demolish strongholds.

"Therefore, go and make disciples of all nations, baptizing them in the name of the Father and of the Son and of the Holy Spirit, and teaching them to obey everything I have commanded you. And surely, I am with you always, to the very end of the age."

—Jesus Christ of Nazareth

A Good Day Every Day

I look out at an infant day, new sun cresting on the trees,
I breathe in the cool peace of early morn—God's creation I perceive.
I taste the new, fresh sweetness in the air,
God's gracious gifts for us all to share.
I thank him for another day as it begins,
Renewed, freed, delivered from all sins.
Blessed to feel the cool freshness in a morning breeze,
To hear the chirping bluebirds nesting in the trees.
I am happy to awake, excited by this new day,
Just as an eager child wants to rush out to play.
And yet as this day unfolds, I know,
I will walk through the high and low.
But come what may, hell or high water,
I will calmly stay focused on my Lord and Savior.
Yes, indeed it surely is a blessed day,
For I am alive with God's gift of life today.
I look forward with wonder to every new morn,
The fathomless joy God gives, with each new dawn.

Matthew 6:34 KJV

Take therefore no thought for the morrow for the morrow shall take thought for the things of itself, sufficient unto the day is the evil therefore.

Psalm 118:24 NLT

This is the day the Lord has made,
we will rejoice and be glad in it.

Psalm 68:19 KJV

Blessed be the Lord, who daily loadeth us with benefits, even the God of our salvation. Selah.

Numbers 6:24—26 KJV

The Lord bless thee and keep thee.
The Lord make his face to shine upon thee and be gracious unto thee.
The Lord lift up his countenance upon thee and give thee peace.

"To be awake is to be alive."

—Henry David Thoreau

I See—Through the Eyes of his Word

Take off the blinders when you read God's word,
If your eyes are covered, the message will be blurred.
Ask the Holy Spirit to behold with God's awesome sight,
To illuminate his words of life, in a spiritual light.
Living life with inner darkness would surely cease,
Spiritual blindness will be replaced by God's guiding light to peace.
Open your spiritual eyes, let the blinding scales fall away,
Watch and listen for the Lord as he speaks to you today.
Let his words of light enter as you open the spiritual door,
And live your life illuminated, in God's wisdom forevermore.

Luke 1:79 NIV

To shine on those living in darkness and in the shadow of death,
to guide our feet into the path of peace.

Acts 9:18 ESV

And immediately something like scales fell from his eyes, and he regained his sight. Then he rose and was baptized.

Psalm 119:105 KJV

Thy word is a lamp unto my feet and a light to my path.

Luke 11:34 NLT

Your eye is like a lamp that provides light for your body. When your eye is healthy, your whole body is filled with light. But when it is unhealthy, your body is filled with darkness.

Proverbs 23:26 NLT

O my son, give me your heart. May your eyes take delight in following my ways.

"I have a fundamental belief in the Bible as the Word of God, written by those who were inspired. I study the Bible daily."

—Isaac Newton

Happy

When I am feeling lonely or my heart feels very sad,
I call upon my Jesus and that makes me feel so glad.
Happy in my heart I am—for Jesus loves me and I know—
That all I have to do is ask and feel his warming mercy flow.
Just knowing that I am not alone and this is not the end,
Brings great joy to my heart, for I have Jesus as a friend.
For if we trust in Jesus and put full faith in him,
He surely will light up our lives if we believe and let him in.
Open your heart and soul today, let his peace and joy flow through.
You will never feel sad or lonely when he shines his love on you.
HAPPY!

Philippians 4:4 NIV

Rejoice in the Lord always. I will say it again; Rejoice!

1 Peter 3:14 KJV

But and if ye suffer for righteousness sake, happy are ye
and be not afraid of their terror neither be troubled.

Psalm 119:1—2 NLT

Joyful are people of integrity, who follow the instructions of
the Lord. Joyful are those who obey his laws and search for
him with all their hearts.

Colossians 1:11 ESV

Being strengthened with all power, according to his glorious might, for all endurance and patience with joy.

"Where your pleasure is, there is your treasure,
where your treasure is, there is your heart,
Where your heart is, there also, is your happiness."

—Augustine

The Church of Mankind

We preach and listen to the messages of Brotherhood and Love,
We praise, we sing, and claim to worship the same God above.
But while we live this test of life, we fail so miserably,
Why will we not love one another as Christ says we ought to be?
So, we choose to keep on living, this charade we all call life,
Immersed in cloaked hatred, open warfare, enmity and strife.
Imagine if we got to Heaven and found out that God is black,
Would you storm out of Paradise; try to find your own way back?
And what if we stood face to face with God and saw that He is red?
Would you opt for a place in Hades, with the eternal dead instead?
We are the body of Jesus Christ, from him the church was born,
So why do we see each other differently, in a temple, on sabbath morn?
Yet while we work side by side, all for a common goal each day,
Your hostility tears me down– upon my very life you flay away.
My heart hurts from the things you say as I feel the loathe you bring,
I wonder how you can stand in church to praise the Lord— to sing.
This malice killed our Savior, yes, we hung him from a tree,
Remember Cain and Abel; mankind's curse—You see?
Imagine what The Messiah felt, as we beat and tore at him.
When we struck and stripped, and humiliated HIM— crucified for OUR sin?
God's love looked down from the cross that day, to save us, you and me,
When Jesus was nailed upon a tree; God freed us ALL for eternity.
Fast forward, two thousand plus years later, will we ever get the message?
The curse lives on, yet we think we have a safe ticket to heaven's passage.
We must awake from our self—righteousness, our holier than thou sleep,
Learn to love, embrace mankind, for we are all God's sheep.
God commands we love one another, that means you and me,
And if we cannot break the curse, there will be no Mankind, no Unity.
With two millenniums passing by it is so hard to change our old ways,

But we do not have too much time left, we must learn to love today.
We have to make peace with our brothers, as we near the last mile of our race,
If we are to hear God say "well done My Child" when you look upon his face.

Galatians 3:28 KJV

There is neither Jew nor Greek, there is neither bond nor free.
There is neither male or female, for ye are all one in Jesus Christ.

Hebrews 12:14-15 NIV

Make every effort to live in peace with everyone and to be holy; without holiness no one will see the Lord. See to it that no one falls short of the grace of God and that no bitter root grows up to cause trouble and defile many.

Psalm 133:1 KJV

Behold how good and how pleasant it is for brethren to
dwell together in unity.

John 15:12—13 NLT

This is my commandment; Love each other in the same way I
have loved you. There is no greater love than to lay down one's
life for one's friends.

1 Corinthians 12:12—14 NIV

Just as a body, though one, has many parts, but all its many parts form one body, so it is with Christ. For we were all baptized by one Spirit so as to form one body, whether Jews or Gentiles, slave or free; and we were all given the one Spirit to drink. Even so the body is not made up of one part but of many.

The Church of Mankind

"The world is my country—all mankind are my brethren and to do good is my religion."

—Thomas Paine

Real Living—In the Spirit

I thank you for the breath of life, that made me a living soul,
The gift of life, of great price, the divine and priceless pearl.
I pledge to live a worthy life—to let your will be done,
I yearn to see your Holy Face when my life's course has been run.
For what is my life worth to me upon this planet earth—
Without the breath of your living spirit, right from my very birth?
My life, my soul and all I am; everything belongs to you,
Help me to be holy and live to be forever true.

Genesis 2:7 KJV

And the Lord God formed a man of the dust of the ground and breathed into his nostrils the breath of life and the man became a living soul.

Matthew 6:10 ESV

Your kingdom come, your will be done, on earth as it is in heaven.

Matthew 13:45—46 KJV

Again, the kingdom of heaven is like unto a merchant man, seeking goodly pearls:
Who, when he had found one pearl of great price, went and sold all that he had, and bought it.

Psalm 27:13 NLT

Yet I am confident I will see the Lord's goodness while I am here in the land of the living.

"True Religion is Real Living, it is living with all one's soul, with all one's goodness and righteousness."

—Albert Einstein.

Restored—Why I Sing Praises

I sing my praise to Jesus for he delivered me from sin,
And through his gift of salvation, I have peace within.
Each day I see his mercy, blessed to live within his grace,
I will live to please my savior until the day I see his face.
He forgives my sins, renews my strength, restores me every day,
I am delivered from eternal death, alive again to say—
"I will love and praise my Jesus until my dying day."
My dreams, fears, hopes and failures—to him I always bring,
His love forever blooms, to restore my everything.
God's touch completely healed my tired broken soul,
His grace restores my life, I am made completely whole.
Jehovah's mercy renews my spirit, my body always heals,
    PRAISE JEHOVAH RAPHA!!!
I worship you, I love you, to you alone I bow; I kneel.
I will exalt, give praise and honor you—all of my days,
Forever will I lift my voice to you in thankful, joyful praise.

Psalm 23:3 KJV

He restoreth my soul, he leadeth me in the paths of righteousness for his name sake.

Jeremiah 29:11 NIV

For I know the plans I have for you declares the Lord, plans to prosper you and not to harm you, plans to give you hope and a future.

Jeremiah 33:6 NIV

Nevertheless, I will bring health and healing to it; I will heal my people and will let them enjoy abundant peace and security.

Psalm 81:1 KJV

Sing aloud unto God our strength, make a joyful noise unto the God of Jacob.

"This perfection is the restoration of man to the state of holiness from which he fell, by creating him anew in Christ Jesus, and restoring him to that image and likeness of God which he has lost."

—Adam Clarke

Leave a Legacy of God's Love

Receive an Everlasting Inheritance

Generations of Humanity come, they go—
We watch, and age as time hurtles by;
Welcoming new birth, the rite of passage,
And we say goodbye to those who die.
Memories of loved ones lost along time's way,
Humbly amplifies the fact, no one is here to stay.
Reflections, reminders of kindred souls gone by,
Mirrors our own fleeting mortality as it draws nigh.
We ask the questions, what goodness can we share—
What joy can we give to others while we are here?
How can we bless the souls that come to take our place—
Exemplifying Christ's love—sharing the salvation of God's good grace?
Perhaps before we leave this earth, we can help others break the chains,
Preach love, spread joy through the "Good News," shed someone's pain.
By touching others with God's love, bonding our very souls,
Is to create a divine fellowship across the entire world.
If we want to share an eternal legacy in this life, as we live,
Then all God's living treasures, to others we must give.
To leave this eternal legacy after we too are gone,
We must pass on the Good News—to each generation that is born.
Faith, Love and Hope—Just Pass it on!

Acts 20:35 KJV

I have shewed you all things, how that so laboring ye ought to support the weak and to remember the words of the Lord Jesus Christ how he said, "It is more blessed to give than to receive."

1 Peter 1:4 ESV

To an inheritance that is imperishable, undefiled, and unfading, kept in heaven for you.

Psalm 78:4 KJV

We will not hide them from their children, shewing to the generation to come the praises of the Lord and his strength and his wonderful works that he hath done.

1 Timothy 6:18—19 ESV

They are to do good, to be rich in good works, to be generous and ready to share. Thus, storing up treasure for themselves as a good foundation for the future, so that they may take hold of that which is truly life.

"What you leave behind is not what is engraved in stone monuments, but what is woven into the lives of others."

—Pericles

Stay with Me Forever Lord—Another Prayer

Thanks for the strength you give me,
To still rise above it all.
Thanks for the courage you fill me with,
To do my best, to stand up tall.
I praise you for the love you've shown,
With you I never feel alone.
Thanks for the joy you send my way,
You always take my hurt and pain away.
You clothe me, feed me and renew me,
Your love; that's what has set me free.
You sent your angels to lead me through,
The cold, blind darkness, and the blue.
And most of all I thank you Lord,
For always being there, my God.
I pray, throughout my life you'll stay,
Forever and always.

Jeremiah 23:4 KJV

I will set up shepherds over them which shall feed them and they shall fear no more, nor be dismayed, neither shall they be lacking, saith the lord.

John 14:16 ESV

And I will ask the Father, and he will give you another helper, to be with you forever,

John 3:16 KJV

For God so loved the world, that he gave his only begotten Son, that whosoever believeth in him should not perish, but have everlasting life.

Psalm 37:18 KJV

The Lord knoweth the days of the upright; and their inheritance shall be forever.

"We do not segment our lives, giving some time to God, some to our business or schooling, while keeping parts to ourselves. The idea is to live all of our lives in the presence of God, under the authority of God, and for the honor and glory of God. That is what the Christian life is all about."

—R.C. Sproul.

Princes & Princess'—Children of the Most High

The King has not Forgotten you

You may not think that you are worth,
The regal blessings of a Princess or a Prince,
But through your tender love, your humility,
You were chosen, crowned, way back since.
Servitude and compassion defined your way,
As you helped so many others rise day to day.
Having shared your life, helping others grow,
You think you've lost your time to sow.
You fear your season to reap will come too late,
It seems like there is not much left upon your plate.
Be not dismayed for your King has seen,
Your Crown, it has been long predestined.
So toil on—planting goodness for our Father divine,
Keep serving in humility, it's okay to toe the line,
On the day you sit with the king at his table to dine,
You'll reap his abundance and drink from his wine.

Note:
Be happy and see the following scriptures as we toil and wait
and do not worry about what's left on your plate.

Matthew 6:31—33 KJV

Therefore, take no thought saying, what shall we eat, or what shall we drink, or wherewithal shall we be clothed?
For your heavenly father knoweth that ye have need of all these things. But seek ye first the kingdom of heaven and all these things shall be added unto you.

Jeremiah 32:19 ESV

Great in counsel and mighty in deed, whose eyes are open to all the ways of the children of man, rewarding each one according to his ways and according to the fruit of his deeds.

Isaiah 25:6 NIV

On this mountain the Lord Almighty will prepare a feast of rich food for all peoples, a banquet of aged wine, the best of meats and the finest of wines

Psalm 113:7—8 KJV

He raiseth up the poor out of the dust and lifteth the needy out of the dunghill. That he may set him with princes, even with the princes of his people.
He maketh the barren woman to keep house and to be a joyful mother of children. Praise ye the Lord.

"Men lose all the material things they leave behind them in this world, but they will carry with them the reward of their charity and alms they give. For these, they will receive from the Lord the reward and the recompense they deserve."

—FRANCIS OF ASSISI

Do Not Ever Forget God

When God's streams of favor on us are flowing good,
With countless blessings, life blooming as it should,
We carelessly let go of God's mighty sustaining hand,
Forgetting the Lord and placing our trust in man.
We should always remember where we are going,
Where we came from and what we used to be.
Yet when life is good, just flowing fine, abundantly,
We ditch heartful praise and thanks and we toss humility.
How quickly God is forgotten, the prayers and talks we had,
The long and hopeless yesterdays, all then so very sad.
Remember how we would ask him to lead us day by day,
And morning, noon and night we would kneel to him, to ask and pray?
That's how we got here, BLESSED, focused on God's face,
Delivered, riding, feeding on his almighty grace.
Friend, do not forget your Savior, do not lose your way,
Get back on your knees again, give praise and thanks today.
Never forget; be thankful, praising God as we run the race,
Keep on living in his salvation and in his ever—saving grace.
*It's the only way to really live. *

Deuteronomy 8:11 KJV

Beware that thou forget not the Lord Jehovah thy God, in not keeping his commandments and his judgements and statutes, which I command this day

Do Not Ever Forget God

Psalm 9:10 NLT

Those who know your name trust in you, for you, O Lord,
do not abandon those who search for you.

Psalm 77:11 NLT

But then I recall all you have done, O Lord; I remember your wonderful deeds of long ago. They are constantly in my thoughts. I cannot stop thinking about your mighty works.

Psalm 78:7 ESV

So that they should set their hope in God and not forget the works of God, but keep his commandments.

Psalm 103:2 NLT

Let all that I am praise the Lord; may I never forget the good things he does for me.

"When to the cross I turn my eyes, and rest on Calvary,
O Lamb of God, my sacrifice, I must remember Thee."

—James Montgomery

In Search of the Great I AM

Look Around—Up and Down

I looked for God upon the Earth, the land, the sky, the sea.
As I pondered in my spirit search, it finally dawned on me,
God IS the world, he made everything, the sea, moon, sun and stars,
Yes, if you have a good telescope, take a long good look at Mars.
God IS, he exists in everything, he made it just for me and you.
The great I AM he is alive in you—he exists in all that's true.
So, the next time you search for him, just take a good long look at you.

John 14: 20 KJV

At that day ye shall know that I am in my Father,
and ye in me, and I in you.

Jeremiah 29:13 NLT

If you look for me wholeheartedly, you will find me.

Isaiah 42:5 ESV

Thus, says God, the Lord, who created the heavens and stretched them out, who spread out the earth and what comes from it, who gives breath to the people on it and spirit to those who walk in it:

"Those who leave everything in God's hand will eventually see God's hand in everything."

—Anonymous

THANX

I praise you for this new day as I awake upon my bed.
Thank you, my Lord Jesus, for the roof above my head.
I humbly thank you Master for the food I have to eat,
I praise you again my Savior for the shoes upon my feet.
Father I offer heartfelt thanks, for the chariot which I ride,
The dry clothes upon my back and your grace to brace the tide.
Let an angel fly before me, as I go out in the world today,
And bring me home safely, steering clear out of harm's way.
Thanks for friends and family, for helping us all to thrive,
For the blessings of peace and joy, your mercies in our lives.
Help me to share love and hope with people that I meet,
To honor your commandments; and your laws, to always keep.
Thank you, Lord.

Philippians 4:6 KJV

Be careful for nothing, but in everything, by prayer and supplication, with thanksgiving let your requests be made known unto God.

Hebrews 13:15 NLT

Therefore, let us offer through Jesus a continual sacrifice of praise to God, proclaiming our allegiance to his name.

1 Thessalonians 5:18 KJV

In everything give thanks, for this is the will of God in Christ Jesus concerning you.

THANX

Psalm 117:1—2 NLT

Praise the Lord all you nations. Praise him, all you people of the earth. For his unfailing love for us is powerful; the Lord's faithfulness endures forever. Praise the Lord!

"O Lord, who lends me life, lend me a heart replete with thankfulness."

—William Shakespeare

Walking Hand in Hand—With God

Awake every morning reach out to God in prayer.
And when you talk to him, believe he will see and hear.
Ask him for guidance, direction; to light your path today,
Walk and talk with him through life's narrow way.
Remember, when you live life in God's mighty shadow,
He will shelter you always, as you bask in his shade—
His awesome peace, infinite love, will never, ever fade.
Keep trusting in the savior, as you walk through this arid land,
Enjoying his richest blessings, walking with him—hand in hand.

Micah 6:8 NIV

He has shown you, O mortal, what is good. And what does the Lord require of you? To act justly and to love mercy and to walk humbly with your God.

Deuteronomy 5:33 KJV

Ye shall walk in all the ways which the Lord your God hath commanded you, that ye may live and that it may be well with you, and that ye may prolong your days in the land that ye shall possess.

Isaiah 41:10 NLT

Don't be afraid, for I am with you. Don't be discouraged, for
I am your God. I will strengthen you and help you.
I will hold you up with my victorious right hand.

Isaiah 41:13 KJV

For I the Lord thy God will hold thy right hand, saying unto
thee fear not, I will help thee.

"Commit yourself to God! He will be your guide. He Himself will travel with you, as it was said He did with the Israelites, to bring them step by step across the desert into the promised land. Ah! what will be your blessedness, if you will but surrender yourself into the hands of God, permitting Him to do whatever He will, not according to your own desires, but according to His own good pleasure?"

—FRANCOIS FENELON

www.ingramcontent.com/pod-product-compliance
Lightning Source LLC
Chambersburg PA
CBHW051053160426
43193CB00010B/1174